Where There is Love, There is No Gender

Where There is Love, There is No Gender

Understanding Love, Sex & Relationships

Dee Weldon Bird

Strategic Book Publishing and Rights Co.

Strategic Book Publishing & Rights Co., LLC
USA | Singapore
www.sbpra.net

For information about special discounts for bulk purchases, please contact Strategic Book Publishing and Rights Co. Special Sales, at bookorder@sbpra.net.

ISBN: 978-1-950860-93-7

AUTHOR'S NOTE

This book is not an autobiography.

It is a book about love.

I have used moments in my life and used them as examples to help explain how love is in everything.

I touch on what I have experienced being mentally and physically abused, I share how religion has played a part in my upbringing as well as being in the institution of social services, as well as growing up being psychic and able to see dead people as it is often called.

All these experiences are love whether tough love or kind love, no matter how you look at it – it's all still love.

Love is not always handled with love and care.

Love is all you need and is unique as you are.

Love covers everything, and so to keep the book simple I touch on my life as a guide.

LOVE IS AS UNCONDITIONAL AS YOU ARE

Experiencing love on Earth physically is different from experiencing love in the universe.

In your soul you are free from physical limitations.

Your soul understands the bigger picture of love.

The physical side of love sees and feels what it wants to know.

Your soul sees and knows everything from all sides and angles at once.

Your soul knows things that the physical puzzles over.

A soul who is experienced in love will understand that it's not about just one way, as life is multifaceted.

Physical experience starts with the self and expands into sharing from the self.

The battles begin when actions do not match up with intentions or words spoken. The physical self may feel threatened, protecting and fighting for its way or no way.

So the battle between physical relationships begin out of self- preservation.

Completion and satisfaction come from the commitment to the self. Facing and holding truth is mastering your experiences in strength and not fear.

No love is more important than another − love is about understanding the depth and meaning. LOVE is as multifaceted as you are which is why you have the ability to change your mind more than once.

You are love – you can be whatever you want to be. Love is not material and it is not just flesh. It is your energy which creates your ideas, your goals, your desires and your passions. Love covers everything.

Your soul gets the bigger picture – it's your physical that is on catch up trying to piece everything together.

Enjoy this book about love. It's full of experiences. A true story – my story.

You will notice throughout this book that certain words are CAPITALIZED. This is to emphasis how LOVE covers EVERY emotion in detail from both sides and all angles.

www.deeweldonbird.com

ACKNOWLEDGEMENTS

I would like to thank every physical soul that has crossed my path literally or remotely. Without experience I would have not remembered everything.

What I have faced in you, I reflected my truth. I have not always been understood. I have been feared. I have experienced how limited physical love can be.

I have experienced the totality of love through the soul where there are often no words in which to physically explain it.

Feelings are your unique pathway in life. Some souls try to merge together as one – this can cause disharmony because of space around every frequency.

The love you share is created from your own signature frequency that you call your essence or your vibe.

I am as thankful for diversity as I am with comfort. I thank my family for accepting my love in me as I accept them.

Love is magical when you remove the veil of the physical flesh. I see you. Do you really see me?

When you see love in its pure form, you then can close your eyes and let go of your physical senses, as your soul sees what the physical is unable to see.

Thank you for sharing your loving space with me as I share my loving space with you.

TABLE OF CONTENTS

INTRODUCTION

LOVE GOT ME TO WHERE I AM TODAY

Love is not something new – you are infinite, total knowing from point zero. My previous book *The Map of The Universe; A Traveler's Guide*, explains everything about point zero. Your soul contains everything – even if you cannot remember. Nothing gets deleted in the Universe.

Love is a vibration of energy – which is why you often say *I feel your vibe*.

What feels new is how you have chosen to experience and express it.

You may ask why has our soul expanded from point zero when we already know everything?

The reason and meaning is this …

What is the point in knowing everything without experiencing it! Knowing is like the manuscript of the universe the script that every soul is connected to.

What you do with that knowing is down to your own free will and choice.

What happens in your soul stays in your soul because of space around each frequency.

You may wonder, *what is the universe?* The universe is space; your signature space within universal space is your soul home you could say.

How you manage your space is up to you. You will notice when there are crowds of people together, that everyone likes their own space.

Looking up at the night sky is often called outer space.

Space IS everything. Without space, nothing would make sense.

You have space between letters, space between words. Space is everywhere. Your soul expands and it contracts.

Your soul is infinitely vast as it is compact.

Your space is like a blank page continuously giving you space to be you.

There are no mistakes or crossings out in your space.

What you create in your space belongs to you and anything past you is a reflection.

You are FREE as well as SAFE in your space in your soul.

You do not lose or forget anything. You do not need to hold on to anything or have fear of being rejected. You are LOVE, accepted and connected in the universe.

There is not judgment or isolation or punishment in the universe.

What you class as punishment is your own understanding of your experience.

How you paint your own picture is totally up to you.

BEFORE CONNECTION WITH
MY PHYSICAL BIRTH

Looking back at my physical map before I connected with earth, I UNDERSTOOD why my first forty years would be full of TRAUMA, FEAR and extreme challenges. My life at four years old became apocalyptic. I lost everything overnight. I knew in my soul that those first forty years of my physical experiences were going to be INTENSE and hard.

The harsh conditions of my life matched the harsh conditions on earth.

I had a crash course on what life had been like for centuries.

A constant REPEAT of abuse and neglect, I had a choice to not turn the outward neglect on my self.

In order to do that. my journey would start in the SEARCH of LOVE WITHIN myself.

Fear had been the driving force for centuries on earth, until the SHIFT that happened March/April of 2018. Love STRENGTHENED from souls that were REMEMBERING who they are.

Love is the completed signature frequency on earth; souls that matched earth's signature frequency would stay. Those that did not would leave earth and connect with a location that matched them.

Earth had been like a hotel for centuries, a hotel that is now closed.

The DISTORTION is over the love frequency of earth is in the driving seat now.

The physical delay of repeated limitation is over. It is all about the SOUL now.

You will remember that you are more than your physical body. You are a power unto yourself; how you harness and express your energy is up to you.

Each soul has self –responsibility. No matter what you experience, your energy leads you back to you.

The map of the universe is within you and everywhere so no soul gets lost.

Your love in you guides you like a beacon even if you cannot see ahead.

Your soul is never in the dark; it is your light.

This IMPACTED me when I looked at my physical map.

I didn't see the doom and gloom and DARKNESS. What I saw is my LIGHT in me always shining.

This is the POWER of love; you CANNOT DESTROY an ENERGY that you cannot physically hold.

This would be like PUNCHING at the air around you.

I knew I was SAFE in my own love balloon within my space no matter what.

I knew that to get through those forty years I had to follow my UNDERSTANDING, which would open doors for me.

I knew following others would CONFUSE my path ahead and lead me to my own physical distortion.

With my map of knowledge safe in my soul, I knew my soul had my physical back.

I knew I always had the connection to the universe and would visit it and be visited in love and support when I needed it.

Even if I felt PHYSICALLY ALONE, my soul knew I was not.

I connected with Earth SCREAMING; in TRUTH I did not want to come to earth.

I was comfortable knowing my path ahead but, like I have said, it's one thing KNOWING it but it is a whole new ball game EXPERIENCING it.

I knew every DETAIL and knew I would not get a breather until forty years later.

This is where my story of love begins before I entered earth.

It was not about PRESERVING the love of myself it was about SHARING my love with you so each SOUL that I met on earth would FEEL their LOVE for themselves.

I remembered early in my CHILDHOOD that seeing is not in the believing – FEELING is.

I felt every step I took on earth, and I equally felt your steps that I observed.

This book is not a self -help book, as you do not need saving. This book is all about UNDERSTANDING LOVE, as understanding is all you need.

CHAPTER ONE

BIRTH – FOUR YEARS

Taking my FIRST BREATH on earth was not easy, as my lungs felt TIGHT and RESTRICTED. Over the weeks, my physical body got STRONGER and the day came when I was able to leave the hospital with my parents. My parents equally had their CHALLENGES. You see, I was a total SURPRISE so they hadn't had a chance to PREPARE for me.

My mother had been told that she wasn't pregnant, that she was just going through menopause. "The Change" as it was called.

My dad was twenty years older than my mum with grown up children of his own, another child was the last thing on his mind.

I did arrive on a special day; it was the day of my niece's 18th birthday.

I was born an aunt. One TITLE of many.

My dad's HEALTH wasn't very good and my mum had schizophrenia, a challenge in itself. The first year was a BLUR. At one year old, I did not only CELEBRATE my BIRTHDAY, my bags were being packed. It was time for me to leave.

My mum was not able to look after me so my dad decided to PAY for foster care. He was not able to take care of me because he had to work.

My mum got admitted to HOSPITAL so they could work out how to manage her ILLNESS.

My dad KISSED me GOODBYE and said, "See you at the weekend". His words were just SOUNDS that I did not understand the MEANING of.

That was to be the ARRANGMENT for the next YEAR.

I would live with the foster parents during the week and stay with my parents at the weekend. A few months later, my mum got DISCHARGED from the hospital. The medication helped to STABILIZE her.

With Mum now at home full-time, my dad wanted me to live back at home full- time too. He had been concerned that I was getting confused who my parents were between them all.

At two years old, I moved back home and I returned on a Sunday to the smell of a lovely roast beef dinner cooking in the kitchen. I walked into the kitchen with my head barely reaching the handle of the kitchen cupboard. I stood next to my mum as I could see that she was carving the joint of beef. With my hand outstretched, I made a sound for a piece and she gave me one. I placed the warm slice in my mouth as I walked out of the kitchen into the lounge, CONTENT until dinner was served.

At times, big adults visited us. I didn't know who they were. I just knew that they were FAMILY. I observed everyone chatting, different emotions that I felt I didn't understand.

Observing my parents I noticed how different they were.

The love I felt from my dad came from within him, in his tone of voice, the way he held my hand and with the look of love in his eyes.

My mum on the other hand was UNTOUCHABLE and UNREACHABLE.

Yes, she was practical in a daily way but it was basic at that. Everyday tasks became a STRUGGLE. I would be placed in the pram for hours in the day to give my mum some space.

My mum would eat lots of chocolates while I got fed custard, anything for an easy life with a demanding nearly-three-year-old. I did not gain weight, which became a concern for my dad and my half sister and her daughter. My half sister would have me stay with her and her daughter to try and feed me up. It was in a yoyo situation. I would get fed properly only to be back to square one when I returned back home.

This caused TENSION within the family.

My mum was not loved much by the family because my dad had moved on too quickly when his first loving wife died. The family felt his decision to marry my mum was a REBOUND in GRIEF, which he DENIED.

My mum was in a stable condition and noticed that my dad had a cough that would not go away. My dad is my world; he bought me toys that were way beyond my years, all stored in the conservatory waiting for me to catch up with them. Looking back, he must have known that he only had two short years with me.

My dad exited the earth just past my second birthday. The following thirteen months seem a blur. All I remember is that my dad's death to me felt left OPEN. I had not had a chance to say GOODBYE.

No one had sat down to explain to me where dad had gone; to me he had just disappeared off the face of the earth. All I had left were my MEMORIES.

I held on to those memories, replaying them constantly so I would not forget his love he shared with me. The love we SHARED would be my first TASTE of love that stayed with me for LIFE; I would later realize that love is more than a memory.

I placed the love I shared with my dad safely inside my love balloon within myself.

No one could see my love balloon and so no one could destroy it; it was as invisible as my dad had physically become. I now had

3

an ANCHOR of love inside myself. It made my tummy feel WARM inside. I felt SAFE knowing I wasn't alone while I felt his love inside of me.

Christmas was soon upon us, with the tree lights glistening; my mum and I sat down in the lounge to watch some TV before it was time for me to go to bed. I stood up on the sofa to reach for the biscuit barrel that was on the sideboard behind the sofa.

It was too heavy for me to hold and my mum held it while opening the lid so I could take a biscuit.

I sat back down in the DARKENED ROOM, with only the light of the TV shining back at us. I suddenly turned to my mum and said, "Mum, you will never DIE will you?"

My mum replied, "NO, I wont." I received her answer loud and clear.

I TRUSTED the words my mum had just said to me.

I BELIEVED her with all my heart and soul.

So I went to bed with a big smile not on my face but inside my tummy.

My mum tucked me up in to bed and as I rested my head onto the pillow, my thoughts replayed our conversation over and over.

"You will never die will you, Mum?"

"No, I will not."

A few days later on the 19th of December, I felt excited as I knew Father Christmas would be arriving soon.

"Not long now," my mum said as she kissed me goodnight.

The next morning I went in to my mum's room to wake her up.

Climbing up on to her bed was a CHALLENGE in itself; it was so high for my little legs. I held on to the covers and pulled myself up.

I said, "Wake up, Mum" as I climbed over her body.

No reply. Nothing!

I climbed on top of her body so my face faced hers. I held her face in my hands asking her to wake up. I could feel my HEART beating faster; I could not work it out.

At first I was CONFUSED as it wasn't normally this hard to wake her up. I opened her eyelids with my tiny fingers and it was at this moment I INSTINCTIVELY knew.

I stared at my LIFELESS mum's physical body and realized I was physically ALONE; as we only lived in this house together.

I now knew she was DEAD. My soul in me knew and told me the truth, my physical part of me was confused and in disbelief. My mum had only just told me that she would never die. I trusted and believed what she said to me, so my mum could not be dead. My mum would not LIE to me.

I CRIED with every BREATH I took, my tears washing my mums face. I chose at that moment not to believe what I physically saw. I thought if I cried enough my ENERGY would TRANSFER into my mum, like when you blow up a balloon to bring it to life.

I wanted to believe that my mum would wake up while my soul deep down told me the truth. Although I stared at death in the face, physically speaking, I knew I could still FEEL her alive.

I don't know how long I was alone with my mum. Eventually our neighbour opened the front door with the spare key that she had. It must have been a sight she will never forget.

Soon family members arrived and a doctor. The doctor confirmed what my soul had been trying to tell me in INSTINCT all along. This truth made me feel dead inside too. That Christmas was frozen not in time but EMOTION, emotions that would take me years to process. For now I stored them not in my love balloon but in my physical tummy.

I could not store them in my mind, as I needed a clear space in my mind to survive.

My tummy was the only spare space I had in my physical body. The words spoken from my mum and the truth that I now faced did not match, and so my battle was to always find out the truth regardless of what words I heard.

My journey of SELF DISCOVERY had begun with nothing but my love balloon to hold on to.

I trusted that love is all I needed.

My life CHANGED overnight.

I had to be BRAVE and GROWN UP like the adults.

After all, I did live in an adult world.

My familiar family became strangers to me as I was to myself. I went within to find my safe space where my love balloon was.

I felt INVISIBLE like my dad and it became my go to space when I wanted to HIDE from the world. I could zone out whenever I wanted and no one knew where I went.

I looked there but not most would say I looked to be in a daze or in a daydream.

I knew where I was SAFE within my space.

Those first few weeks staying in foster care were like a pause button on my life; I was totally SWITCHED OFF from here. Then a man I vaguely knew, as he had visited my mum a few times in our kitchen, came to pick me up. No warm welcome, he just PUSHED his flat hand on my back and told me to get into his car while he loaded it up with my things. I stared out of the window and could see my breath on the car window. I could smell the air outside. It smelt nothing like back at home.

The car stopped outside a big house. I could see lots of open fields and animals.

Walking inside I knew that I wasn't going to be happy here as I could SENSE I wasn't wanted. Those six months were a living HELL which I shared with you in my first book, *From Both Sides of The Fence – The Gifts in U.*

I thought finding my mum dead was going to be the worst it would get but it wasn't.

I had already known what it was like to feel extreme HUNGER. You get used to it after awhile. What you cannot control, you tend to accept and surrender to.

This is what I did.

I was only four years old, just a child. Straight away it was obvious how being a child around adults I didn't have much of a voice. Shut up and put up with it.

It depended if they where INVESTED in you or in themselves.

I had already faced two deaths. I then faced being starved, followed by being WHIPPED and SEXUALLY ABUSED.

I wrote about this in my first book *From Both Sides of The Fence; The Gifts in U.*

To be HONEST it was lucky my life started how it was to continue, as I certainly didn't have time to get settled or comfortable.

The basics of love had gone out of the window for me.

I felt dead after my mum died and now I felt NUMB. I now felt like a skeleton with its muscles and organs and skin intact.

I was starting to HATE this body as much as others did.

Six months later I was dropped off at a building by a member of my real family I didn't even know where I was. A lady came up to me and said she was a social worker and then she told me her name.

What could I say? She was just a lady to me. This lady said she would be taking me to where I would be staying. I just gave a BLANK STARE. Facing the UNKNOWN didn't feel as scary compared to the fear I had faced in the last six months. I had nothing familiar to physically hold onto apart from the coat on my back.

The lady asked me if she could help me with my coat. I stared her in the face and said, "I can do it myself", as I stamped one foot on the floor. I pulled both sides of my coat together as I fastened the buttons.

I didn't want to be RUDE; I was being PROTECTIVE over the one thing I had left that I had control of, even if it was down to just buttoning up my coat. I still had my SELF-WILL left and that was something. This lady took my hand and showed me to her car.

I didn't really enjoy car journeys as they always made me feel sick. Maybe it was my past emotions that were swimming around in my belly, like shark infested waters.

I was NERVOUS about where I was going and yet had to go with it and face it.

The lady suddenly said, "We are here." We pulled up outside two houses that were detached.

Opposite I could see a long building and a big church behind it. This place was so different to where I had just come from.

"That is called a convent where the nuns stay."

I didn't understand what this lady was saying it went through one ear and out the other. The lady with me rang the doorbell and a woman answered the door with a lovely smile and said her name was Mrs G.

Her smile made me feel more COMFORTABLE as I had not seen one of those for awhile. As I took my first steps through the door, I knew my history of my past was safe in my tummy, not digested like food; just stored there so no one could see it.

SURVIVAL had been my priority, not my emotions or how I felt.

I had swallowed my history and buried it. I DETACHED from my past like it had happened to someone else. The social worker lady introduced me and said, "This is Dorothy. She is just over four years old."

After we had exchanged our hello's, Mrs G showed me where to hang up my coat. We had a drink and went to the bathroom before Mrs G showed me around the children's home.

I didn't even ask what a children's home was, I just ACCEPTED that it was the name of the house and that was it. All the children that lived there were out at school.

That's why I saw lots of coat pegs with names next to them.

Mrs G showed us the kitchen and the garden. We then walked into the dining area and through into the lounge. Walking back past the dining area, we walked past the toilets and past two other rooms that we did not go in.

Opposite the front door were the stairs. We climbed them and after reaching the top of the stairs you could turn right or left onto the landing. We turned left and walked past two bathrooms on our right and big cupboards on our left, and three bedrooms were at the end. Mrs G showed me which bed was mine out of the bedrooms. We walked back past the bathrooms where we were shown the other bedrooms.

Back down the stairs, the lady that brought me told me that she had to go and that Mrs G will look after me now. We said our goodbyes and she left.

I followed Mrs G into the kitchen. I sat on a high stool while I watched her prepare dinner for the children for when they got home from school.

I had only been used to a life with adults; I mixed with other children occasionally when I was living with my mum and dad.

I felt nervous, as I didn't know what to expect.

I stayed QUIET until a man turned up delivering boxes.

Mrs G was busy putting the boxes away, which left me ALONE with this man.

He asked me how old I was.

I said, "I am four."

He said "You will soon be going to school!"

I said, "Not until September, as I will be five by then."

As I sat on a chair waiting, I ZONED OUT into my safe space within myself.

I hadn't experienced labels yet but I had experienced name-calling that made me forget that my birth name was Dorothy.

I suddenly heard my name being called – "Dorothy, come with me to the kitchen as the children are arriving home now."

I watched as many children walked past me of all ages and NATIONALATIES and BACKGROUNDS.

I was too young to know this yet, they were just other children to me in this moment.

I soon slotted in to the routine and got to know all the children in the children's home.

I was in house Nos 95. The house next door was also a children's home. Children from each home didn't mix that much only during outside play if we crossed the path between each home.

I felt safe in the children's home. We were all treated the SAME, no child had more than the other. We each had a bed and a wardrobe and a wooden chair to put our clothes on for the day.

I had SPACE from my emotions and my TRAUMATIC past. I was able to be a child and play like other kids.

I was HAPPY to be able to BREATHE without having to hold by breath for the next beating.

It was hard to get close to people in a bonding way, because kids came and went and staff had shifts. I would say in the moment I had close bonds for how long it lasted in time.

My first taste of being different, past my physical family, was nothing to do with gender or skin colour. It was Uniform. I had never seen anything like it before. The uniform worn by the nuns in the homes and in the convent. They wore long dresses and head-dresses with huge crosses hung around their necks. Us kids thought they looked like penguins because the clothing was black and white.

Like anything new, it is STRANGE at first, once you realize the clothing is not a THREAT and you then see past it. I got to know the nun behind the clothing.

I went to playgroup while the other kids went to school because I was the youngest in the homes. I remember the staff at the playgroup would want us all to have a nap after lunch. There were lots of camp beds and I would PRETEND I was asleep and look around the room through my partially closed eyes. I never UNDERSTOOD why we had to sleep when I was not tired and it wasn't bedtime and it was daytime.

Once school broke up for the summer holidays, we children were ALLOWED to walk to the shops together. One particular day, some of the kids thought it would be a fun idea to steal some sweets from a shop. After doing so, we all got caught, even if we hadn't taken anything.

The police drove us back to the children's home. The policeman told the staff what had happened. Staff lined us up in the lounge and we stood in front of the big fireguard, going down in height and age. I was at the end of the line being the smallest and the youngest.

The policeman walked in with staff and stood in front of us, as he talked to us. It was like the room around me blurred. His voice became muffled as if I was TRANSLUCENT. There, but not.

My physical self was there but the feeling me tuned out this scene. Maybe it was because I didn't really understand what was going on and wondered what the PUNISHMENT would be.

11

I always zoned out into my space when I knew I was going to be punished. His uniform stood out in AUTHORITY and not PRAYER.

Not a lot happened after that. We all went to bed early without getting our toasted buttered crumpet. All of the kids in the homes accepted each other with no JUDGMENT, because we all were in the same boat. I knew I was DIFFERENT because I was the only ORPHAN and the other kids still had family. Through all our different backgrounds we all got on because life outside had been harsh in comparison. I guess you could say it was like a safe house and time out from the harsh realties of the outside world.

My first birthday in the homes was confusing because staff didn't have my birth certificate and they didn't know if it was the 16th or 17th August, so they took a guess and it was celebrated on the 16th. Birthdays were not a big deal; it just meant you went up a number. They later found out it was the 17Th so no more early birthdays for me.

OVERVIEW

Looking back over those first four years of my life, I experienced how love can feel FRAGILE, but how STRONG it is at the same time. Don't get me wrong, I had been stripped bare past being naked and abused. I had been stripped of my self-identity and I had swapped it out with many names along the way that best described me in that moment.

I had lost more than my family. I had lost my sense of self-belonging, having no roots to settle in. I was out of my depth from the get go and knew my life would not be shallow and easy to paddle in. My life started out as it meant to go on, deep and intense, not out of my own making. I just wanted to be loved and happy rather than rejected and passed from pillar to post.

I was lost in an adult world that I found SOLACE in when I was able to mix with kids in the next chapter of my life.

LOVE is not BLACK or WHITE or rich or poor, it had so far been a long road in a short few years of self discovery in situations and circumstances that would make the story of my life come ALIVE. Not a love story but my story, how I searched for love, the MISSING piece inside of me.

Love that I SEARCHED for is what I called my love balloon that I carried with me always. Invisible to others but VISIBLE to me, some would go on to say that I wore my love on my sleeve. It showed that not matter what, love was my guide no matter how dark and bleak my life got. Love would always be my reason and meaning behind every step that I took, whether I travelled light or heavy or blind or on autopilot, in planned knowing or no preference, love was always by my side.

CHAPTER TWO

5 – 10 YEARS

Those first few months I was just settling into life in the homes. Now my life would EXPAND out into the world, when I started at the Infants School around the corner. All us kids walked together every morning as it was literally at the back of our house out of the back gate. I lined up to go into class in the infants while the other kids went to the other side in the juniors. I already knew some of the kids as the staff children went to the same school.

School was FUN as they had lots of toys to play with. Infants didn't really IMPACT me. It was just a place to go during the day. I lived in an INSTITUTION with routine, which ran like clockwork. The day started by getting up and dressing ourselves and making our own beds. We where taught how to make them with folded corners, as one of the staff had been a nurse and showed us. Lucky for me I was not on a top bunk being only small. How the older kids made theirs I didn't know.

After we had brushed our teeth and washed, we all met in the big dining room for our breakfast. There were rows of tables with lots of cutlery and different coloured boat shaped eggcups. I chose a red eggcup. Each day was the same. We had cereal followed by a boiled egg and a cup of tea. We certainly didn't go to school HUNGRY.

I started to OBSERVE more the older I got. I was now DRIFTING far away from my past, something I didn't want to be reminded of, as this was my life now.

However, one particular weekend I was to be reminded that even in the homes, I was the ODD one out. All the children were excitedly packing their bags to go home to their families for Christmas but not me. I didn't have a family anymore. All I could do was watch them. I didn't even know where they were all going or what a back home was. I just accepted that this is how my life was now. A life of SITUATION and CIRCUMSTANCE; it felt like I was just FOLLOWING a life that I would not have CHOSEN.

As each child left, the children's home felt BIGGER as I was the only one left behind.

I could hear staff talking with the head nun, trying to work out what to do with me for the holidays as the home closed with no children. They could not be EXPECTED to keep the home open just for me. I heard Mrs G say, "Dorothy is WELCOME to spend Christmas with my family."

All the staff agreed and Mrs G took my hand to pack my bag, I had somewhere to go after all.

This was the arrangement over the years; I would stay with Mrs G unless she was busy. That first Christmas surfaced the FACTS; that I was DIFFERENT being the only orphan and that is as far as that TRIGGER went.

I opened a handful of gifts from a black bag; I was so happy that I hadn't become invisible to Father Christmas and FORGOTTEN. It didn't matter what I had opened that Christmas morning, for me the GIFT was about being INCLUDED and not shut out. Being included meant more to me than anything and this MEANING stayed with me through my life. I didn't COMPARE what I had with other kids because whatever you had in the children's homes never just belonged to you. We SHARED everything.

If I had a day out and brought back some sweets, all the kids would gather round as we shared them.

It wasn't the RULES or anything but just a MUTUAL SUBLIMINAL understanding that whatever happened in the homes, we all stuck together. That life was all I knew, of clockwork routine and chores to help us EARN some pocket money. There was nothing to FIGHT over, as we all wanted the SAME thing, to be DISTRACTED from our past PAIN that we carried deep inside. We all just wanted to be FREE from those feelings, and the only way to achieve that was to LAUGH and have FUN.

What normal kids got cross over seemed PETTY to me. I didn't understand why they could be cross or upset. Wasn't being REMEMBERED enough? This happened one Christmas when I watched as a child didn't get the specific toy they wanted, although they had piles of toys that they had already opened.

I never knew that you actually asked Father Christmas for specific toys on a list.

I thought whatever you got is what Father Christmas chose for you. The MAGIC for me was not the toy, it was the fact Father Christmas came. All I could do is watch as her mum tried to COMFORT this OUTBURST of unfairness.

We had our Christmas dinner and after dinner each child got one more gift. As the child opened the last gift, she beamed the biggest smile and got what she wanted after all. I was just thankful that her SADNESS was over; I didn't like how it made me feel WATCHING her DISTRESS. I guess it reminded me of my own tears even if for different reasons. It was my first experience of putting myself in her shoes.

I was starting to know my place in life, and knew that I would never be like normal kids on the outside. People on the outside FEARED us as damaged goods, our only worth was TROUBLE.

As each year passed, each summer holiday was the same. A big detached house at a place called Littlestone in Kent was where children in the homes went and stayed for their summer holiday. Each home had a scheduled week.

It was my turn to see staff; I had to meet them upstairs on the landing by the big built in storage cupboards on the left. The big doors were wide open and staff asked me to take off my shoes so I could try on a pair of plimsolls for the beach. Any clothes that I would need came out of this big cupboard.

We traveled by coach and not the mini bus that was used for day trips. What an ADVENTURE! We sang with big smiles on our faces all the way there. As the coach stopped we could see the big white house that was across the road opposite the sea. We unpacked our bags and walked to the ground floor section of the big house, with many dorms to choose from, each room had wooden floors and walls.

The bathrooms where huge with lots of shower cubicles. The rooms looked quite dim due to being on the ground floor. Once unpacked, staff said we could go outside to play.

Wow! The garden had columns of trees that we could run up and down; it was like entering a MAZE if you used your IMAGINATION. There were many steps from the patio doors and a small level wall so we had plenty of places to sit. There was a flat bit of green before you reached the trees. We would do handstands and have so much fun.

Staff called to say that lunch was ready. They carried big silver catering tea urns and plates of sandwiches outside. We all ate quickly as we wanted to get back to playing. Staff asked if we wanted a cup of tea or water. We all chose tea no matter how old we were.

The owners of the house came down from the top floor to meet us. They were an old couple and very KIND and FRIENDLY. The old man sat on the steps with us and taught us a rhyme that you played out with your fingers. It was something we didn't forget. It was nice that someone from the outside wanting to speak to us. We didn't see them again during the rest of the week that we were there.

We had everything we needed in the homes; kids to play with and food in our bellies and a chance to explore childhood. Everything we needed came from the storage in the homes, the only time we visited the outside world was to go to school or to different activities.

I had to see an optician yearly because I was born with BAD eyes and a squint. I was the only child that had to wear national health glasses, so you could not miss me in the homes. I often had to have a plaster stuck around the arm of the glasses to keep them together until my next visit.

The outside world was not really part of us because we were different. We kept ourselves to ourselves. We visited the outside world in our safe group. I had swimming lessons and would take other children with me to get on two buses to swimming class. Adults didn't come with you. You just had to get on with it. There was no room for fear.

We also went to Saturday morning pictures and did an art craft after in the local town. We would all go together which took up most of the day. Old feelings had not really SURFACED, more practical AWARENESS of my situation and keeping up with the routine.

We went on day trips in the van to pick fruit from the fields. Staff came with us and handed us plastic Tupperware boxes for us each to fill up with blackberries.

Obviously each of us would eat them as well as pick them. We DENIED that we had, even though you could see the blackberry juice around our mouths. This is when I first LEARNT about denying the truth.

It didn't really bother me as I knew the staff knew the truth, the truth was not HIDDEN it was in PLAIN SIGHT, so it made this denial somehow ok. Plus it didn't happen very often. We filled up all the boxes. This fruit became our puddings throughout the winter months.

At seven years old, it was like I was coming back into my own. Those last few years felt like I was spaced out from life. I had visits OCCASIONALY from my niece and I would have a day out to visit my uncle at his house. He had three daughters of his own. They were of similar age to me. My family was just a NAME or a HEADING to me and not close in my personal space. Contact stopped after a few day trips and I didn't see him again and I didn't know why.

I remember he took me to the zoo once and round his local market and he bought us each a beaded necklace. I didn't take it PERSONALLY as I was used to people coming and going in my life. Nothing stayed the same for long. I guess you could say I took it at face value, as nothing impacted my feelings those days like my past did.

I left the children's home from time to time to stay with strangers with their family. I later learned this was being fostered out. I didn't like leaving my friends from the children's home so I didn't make LIFE EASY when I stayed with strangers.

I didn't have a VOICE and if I did my words were not always HEARD. The only way I got the adults ATTENTION was through my ACTIONS.

I made it clear that I was not happy and not settling with these strangers. A social worker soon picked me up to return me back to the children's home and I was happy to see all the familiar faces. The children's home became my familiar family. It is all I knew and felt settled with the practical routine of it all. I saw children LEAVE and RETURN like me. I saw children leave to live back home with their family never to see them again.

I had gotten close to three children in the homes who were part of their own same family. There was a boy the same age as me and two older sisters. They had taken me under their WING you could say. I PHYSICALLY didn't LOOK like them with my bright blonde wispy hair compared to their thick black Afro textured hair. The oldest out of the two girls would plait my hair for me in the mornings so I was ready for school. I would only let her do it if she was FREE.

I loved them all so much! It was like being part of their family and being a sister. It didn't matter to any of us that I looked different from them. We loved each other because we shared life together and our close bond was out of love and not the colour of skin. They let me play with their hair as they played with mine. I accepted why the nun put Vaseline on their hair before going outside in the summer to PROTECT it from the sun. I didn't feel LEFT OUT because I didn't have it on mine. I UNDERSTOOD it was because of our different types of hair. Some things you just accept in MATERIAL and don't take it PERSONALLY. I was amazed by the eldest. She was so beautiful and her art was AMAZING. I loved sitting on her bunk and looking at her work.

I STRUGGLED at school. I had been so used to being in SURVIVAL mode, my brain was taken up with storing my childhood past. I had no spare storage space to retain school work.

My brain was full because I had not FACED my past to create some space for learning. I was classed as UNEDUCABLE.

When I got homework I would find my friend and ask her to HELP me. I was THANKFUL that I always had someone I was able to turn to.

RELIGION was a big part of our routine; we would go to mass during the week and on Sundays. I found it ENTERTAINING as I sat in church. I watched how the priest would fill the church with incense. We would have ash put on our foreheads in the sign of the cross on Ash Wednesday. We never saw chocolate EASTER EGGS, only the boiled egg kind.

Staff would hand us each a rosary to take to church; blue ones for the boys and pink for the girls. They made us feel INVOLVED with what the nuns were doing.

Life wasn't always easy in the homes and living with nuns didn't make it any easier.

The teachers at the school did not LIKE teaching us kids from the homes. I didn't focus on how different we were; I focused on holding my own. What I lacked in material WEALTH I made up in MORALS and MANNERS. When teachers set certain topics it caused me to QUESTION who I was.

One topic we had to do was write out our family tree. Mine was left BLANK and I wrote on the piece of paper, that I was born in a dustbin for all I knew. I had blanked my past out of my mind.

Another day teachers asked us all to bring in a gift to do a lucky dip in class.

Some kids brought in beautifully wrapped gifts. I kept asking staff for my gift that I could bring in, as it was the last day in which to do so. The head nun gave me a packet of sandwich mallows from the food store room. They were wafers with pink and white mallow filling. I wasn't able to wrap them up so staff gave me a paper bag to put them in.

Just after lunch it was time for the class to do the lucky dip. I picked my gift and started to unwrap it and another kid opened mine. I had a box of chocolates and they looked so EXPENSIVE. The child that had opened my sandwich mallows had been the child that had brought in the box of chocolates.

She was not happy to say the least and made it OBVIOUS to everyone. I said she could have her box of chocolates back as it wasn't my fault and I had no choice on what I could bring in. It was sandwich mallows or nothing at all. I remember feeling so BAD for the other child as I could SEE and FEEL how upset and DISAPPOINTED she was. My sandwich mallow gift had made her feel so upset and grumpy. I did not know what the meaning behind this task was, but it wasn't fun.

Don't get me wrong. I felt incredibly LUCKY to have received such a GENEROUS gift in EXCHANGE for what I brought in, but I was unable to ENJOY it. The only way I would feel better was to share them, so I opened up the box of chocolates for the WHOLE class to enjoy.

We had English class with a teacher we called Mrs Wiggleworm as her surname sounded similar. I noticed how this teacher kept PICKING on a particular boy. I could not observe her picking on him any longer; I didn't feel he deserved to be treated like this. I got up out of my seat and walked past the rows of desks to the front of the class to where Mrs Wiggleworm was sitting at her desk. Behind her big glasses that perched on the end of her nose, she looked over the rims at me and asked what I wanted. I kicked her on her shins and told her to leave him alone, to STOP being a BULLY and before I even gave her a chance to speak, I QUIETLY walked back to my desk. She must have been SHOCKED as she did nothing, not even tell me off. It worked though as she never picked on him again after that. The children in class seemed STUNNED into SILENCE also. It all felt like a silent movie as it unfolded, like it was done under the radar, but I had achieved what I had INTENDED; to PROTECT and LOOK OUT for him.

I may have only been seven years old, but my moral ground was starting to show. I felt what others felt. I knew you could either watch and shut up or observe and do something about it. I always chose to stand up and be counted rather than to sit down and bury my head in my hands and ignore.

The boy I had looked out for was so HANDSOME and every girl fancied him. We would play KISS CHASE in the playground. His skin tone was HALF CAST—not that this made any difference. He had looks and that was it. His mum was a nurse and he taught us that babies do not come from your bellybutton but your bum area. We screwed our noses up not wanting to believe him and wanted to stick with the idea of the belly button. Whether we AGREED to DISAGREE, we CARED about each other.

One girl I got close to at school was brought up by her Nan. They lived in a house opposite the school playground and she would often look out to see if she could see her Nan during break. It was during break I told her about my SECRET that I saw people that other people couldn't see. I pointed to an old lady that I could see walking past the school and I asked if she could see her. I knew she would not be able to and she said no that she could not see her. She didn't freak out and just listened without judgment.

Another time I was upset during class and suddenly found myself on the bench in the middle of the playground. As I sat on the bench my back was to the classrooms of the school. I turned my head round to look at everyone in their classes and wondered how I had gotten away with being in the playground when you can see me from the classrooms in plain sight. How had I walked past the teachers to get outside in the first place?

No one came after me – it was like I was invisible and that I was in my REALITY and the school was in theirs. The school bell went and all the kids ran out for break. This event never made sense to me neither did I ever forget it. I either had an OUT OF BODY EXPERIENCE or I became invisible that day. There is no way I would have been allowed to sit there missing class without getting noticed otherwise.

Art at school could be fun at times but extremely challenging. We had to each make a life-sized puppet of ourselves for our next assembly that would be in front of mums and dads.

Each week we worked on our puppets and mine looked AWFUL. I was so EMBARRASSED – there was no way I was showing this during assembly.

The mums and dads started arriving and they all sat on chairs in the hall with the children seated in front of them cross-legged on the floor.

The head of the school introduced us and asked us to stand up to do our play. I followed the kids in front of me and stood in the front row. Most of my class were holding their puppets but I had left mine on the floor where I had been sitting. I felt pleased with my self as I had gotten away without showing my puppet.

Our teacher suddenly noticed that I didn't have my puppet and asked for a teacher to pass it to her to give to me. I wanted the floor to open up and swallow me whole. I was so embarrassed as my puppet was now HIGHLIGHTED for everyone to see.

I tried to hide my puppet as much as I could during our class song. I was so relieved when our assembly was over. I left the puppet at school. I never wanted to see it ever again.

Another evening our class was putting on a gymnastics display for the parents.

Lots of benches were placed in rows for the parents to sit on in the school hall.

Once all the parents were seated, our head teacher introduced our class to them.

I didn't have any parents to watch me. Even the staff were busy with chores they had to do.

I had done the best one-handed cartwheel. No one had done one in our class before.

I was so PROUD of myself, as well as SAD.

Once our display finished, all the parents clapped. The parents rushed over to their children to HUG and KISS them, praising them while getting them dressed, something I could only observe and never experience.

I was so EMBARRASSED. I felt that I stood out for the wrong reasons. I rushed out the back door hoping no one would see me leave. I walked back to the children's home feeling sad that no one watched my one-handed cartwheel display.

Situations like this reminded me and put me in my place that I was an ORPHAN, and no matter how much I tried to fit in, life would remind me that I was different.

The next day at school I had gone from feeling proud of myself for the previous nights gym display to more embarrassment. Why is it that praise would be like bursting a bubble? It never lasted.

At the end of a school day we would put our chairs onto our desk so the cleaners could come in and clean the classroom without the chairs getting in their way.

We would stand behind our desks and wait for the teacher to say an end of day prayer.

I was BUSTING to go to the toilet, no matter how much I crossed my legs the flood gates where going to open. I felt a warm trickle down my legs and my feet felt damp and I now was standing in a pool of my own making.

With my head facing the floor as I walked, it was the only way I knew how to hide my embarrassment. I had to go to the staff room to get a paper bag to put my wet knickers in and the teacher gave me a clean pair to borrow.

I had seen other kids with the tell-tale brown paper bag before so I knew it wasn't just me. I walked so fast back to the homes trying to hide my brown paper bag behind my body.

I didn't dwell on it too much. Thankfully it only happened a couple of times, these ACCIDENTS as it was called. At least I stood out because of an accident rather than the reason for being in the homes.

Being an orphan weighed HEAVY on my mind and living in the children's home highlighted it. It took me three years to save up my pocket money for a Tiny Tears doll that I wanted so badly. Its arms and legs moved and it drank from a bottle, which made it wet its nappy. It was like a REAL baby. I always carried a doll around with me in the children's home. I guess it made me feel less ALONE.

One Christmas, I finally got the Tiny Tears doll. It cried real tears as well as wet its nappy. I loved this doll so much. I would place it at the foot of my bed before I went to sleep and I would pray that it would turn into a real baby during the night. I was DISAPPOINTED that it never happened but I continued loving this doll as if it were real.

Around this age I asked the staff if I could have my ears pierced. I was told I would be able to one day, but it just NEVER happened. I guess it was out of staff's hands.

At least I felt they LISTENED to me during our CONVERSATIONS, even if they could not give me what I would like. I remember the next day the staff nun gave us our dinner money for the week. It cost twelve and a half pence. We also got a half pint of milk with a straw in it at break time. We loved drinking out of them.

I loved school dinners too, so much so that I would spend most of my time going up for more. It wasn't unusual that I had seconds, but this particular day I had thirds. The dinner ladies must have thought that I had hollow legs. They were amazed what I could pack away and they gave me a Barbie type doll. I felt like I had gained an AWARD for simply eating. I had a really full tummy with a big smile on my face, feeling really lucky to have this doll, and the fact it was NAKED didn't bother me.

My three friends that had taken me under their wing were leaving the homes to live back home with their mum full time FOREVER.

I sat at the top of the stairs on a chair with Mrs G and we watched them leave. I had tears rolling down my cheeks. I said to Mrs G, "Why is it that anyone I get CLOSE to either dies or leaves?"

Mrs G did not reply.

I watched as their heads disappeared out of sight. They left and I never saw them again.

I was so thankful they had been so KIND to me and LOVED me like a SISTER.

Life carried on and more children arrived.

I was the longest resident at the children's home.

I would be VISITED by my social worker and over the years I had a male and a few females. One particular day my social worker took me out to a café to have a chat with me over lunch.

As I ate my lunch the social worker told me that a family wanted to foster me. Out of the selection of children, they had CHOSEN me, because I liked to sing and play the recorder.

She went on to say that this family was going to visit me in the children's home to introduce themselves. This family decided they would take me out for the day at the seaside so I could meet their daughter. They had children of their own, two boys and one girl. Their daughter was SHY and they felt if they fostered a girl it would help their daughter to be MORE CONFIDENT.

As I sat in the back of their car, they gave me a boiled sweet to suck on. It was so big that I could barely close my mouth and found it even harder to talk. The first sentence I said to their daughter was, "You're shy ain't ya?

The daughter didn't reply.

I didn't mean to be rude or anything. I just spoke the truth from my observation.

We had a fun day on the beach where I did cartwheels across the sand.

After a few visits, I went to stay with them at their house for the weekend. I had my own bed in a bedroom, something that I had never experienced. They lived in a big house called a rectory because the man was a vicar. It was nice visiting their house but that's all it was: visiting.

This reminded me of when I went round to my friend's house and her bedroom was like an Aladdin's cave. She had a pink bedroom with beautiful bedding and lots of toys and jewelry boxes and beads; it was so magical, a stark difference to our bedroom in the children's home. Our bedroom had dark blue curtains, with a wooden chair and a wooden wardrobe. The only colour we had came from our dressing gowns.

So having my own bedroom to sleep in with the foster family reminded me of my friends' home that I had visited. The family asked if I would like to live with them full time.

I said yes at first because visits had been fun.

The closer it got to leaving the children's home, the more I didn't want to leave.

I told staff that I didn't want to live with this family.

The man of the foster family arrived while I was eating dinner. I was slow as I was in no rush to visit them.

Pudding that day was a bowl of Gooseberries. I can't stand them, the smell of them alone makes my stomach turn. The foster man told me to buck up. I thought to myself, *what is buck up?* I had never heard such words. As silly as this sounds, hearing those words added to why I liked them even less for changing my life.

I stuffed three green balls of gooseberry into my mouth and rushed outside into the back garden to spit them out. They are an acquired taste for sure; we didn't even have custard or anything to help them go down.

The weekend came round too quickly. Being ten, nearly eleven, meant secondary school would soon be upon me.

All the staff that had known me over the years in the children's home turned up to say GOODBYE even if it wasn't their shift.

I had tears rolling down my face, as I wasn't happy to be leaving what had been HOME for me since I arrived at four years old. I had grown up here.

Staff took a picture of me with the kids before I LEFT using an instamatic camera.

I was sad that my voice had not been HEARD. I had told staff so many times that I did not want to leave but it was decided for me. With my bag packed and with a HEAVY heart I sat quietly in the backseat of the car, and I waved goodbye to everyone in the children's home, somewhere that I had BELONGED and called home.

To me it didn't matter where I would live, it would not change that I was an orphan, no matter how much you try and cover it up with different labels.

My only possession left of my childhood roots was my BIRTH NAME Dorothy WELDON. This was what mattered the most to me.

OVERVIEW

Experiencing love during these years was focused on childhood fun and laughter, still keeping my DEMONS at bay and hiding from myself. I could not bare the thought of seeing myself so I certainly didn't want anyone else finding out about me from my past.

Life for me during these years gave me an escape route to be a different me and experience the INNOCENCE of youth without the mitts of adults all over me.

I had my first taste of hope and wishing for something out of choice. A plastic doll to some, but to me a lifeline of belonging to something rather than being on my own. I experienced disappointment and let down. I started to feel like an advent calendar, each day I opened my eyes to reveal a different angle and take on love.

Love had been so far an EXTERNAL INFLUENCE and now the tables where starting to turn as my experiences grew with me personally. Love certainly had gotten my ATTENTION now.

CHAPTER THREE

11 – 18 YEARS

So far love for me hadn't been about NURTURING and COMFORT. It had been about LOSS and TRAUMA with a lot of survival in order to face fear in all new situations. I had not been able to settle and get comfortable. My life so far had been a rollercoaster ride that I had already had enough of and wanted to get off. Maybe this next chapter in my life I would experience love from a whole different angle.

We moved to Harold Hill in Havering in Essex. I sang in the choir during the Christmas service in the church and after the service a lady came up to me.

She asked me if my name was Dorothy Weldon.

I said, "Yes."

She gasped and said, "I thought it was you. I lived next door to your mum and dad and I found you when your mum PASSED."

I arranged to meet at her house; she only lived around the corner to the vicarage.

I went but I found it all too OVERWHELMING. She was pleased to see me after her traumatic experience that day when she found me alone with a dead mum.

She gave me a huge teddy bear, which was one my parents had bought me. She had kept it all these years in her house. I carried this huge teddy back to the vicarage with tears streaming down my face.

I had so many emotions surfacing that I didn't know which to feel the most. I HATED Christmas. It was full of pain and loss that I could not even love this teddy or feel the love in it. It just reminded me of my pain.

I never saw her again after that. It was too RAW selfishly for me; it was nothing personal toward her. A few times I skated on my roller skates past the house I lived in with my real parents. I just hadn't known it yet. Talk about the past come back to haunt me! I was relieved when I found out that we where moving to a place called Loughton in Essex.

I had a lot to get my head around living with a vicar's family. I had switched one religion for another. I wasn't allowed to call it going to mass. I had to now say church. C of E is not the same as a Catholic church. We only had to go on a Sunday and not during the week anymore. I didn't have a rosary and the vicar didn't make the church smell of incense. I did sing in the choir like their children did. I didn't enjoy church as much as mass; it was depressing and concentrated on evil and repenting of sins.

I finished my last term of the juniors at the school my foster woman worked at.

I made some nice friends but found the schoolwork hard as I was in survival mode.

Summer holidays soon came around, and there was no going to Littlestone where I had always gone with the children's home. I got fitted for my school uniform, which had to be altered because I was so little for my age.

I MISSED the children's home and all my friends. I felt cut off from what I had known. My familiar world had changed again like it had years ago. I was told that the head nun didn't want me to be fostered, as other foster homes had not worked. She felt that I had spent too many years in the homes to move now but she reluctantly agreed.

The social worker visited me at the foster family's house. I hardly said a word as I had felt what was the point in talking to these adults when they don't listen to you?

We moved just in time before school started in the summer. I was nervous to start school as I didn't know anyone. At the school gates I walked over to a girl standing on her own and we became close school friends.

The foster family said I had been registered at the school with their surname, so I looked like one of the family. I wasn't happy about not using my birth surname, as it was all I had left from my real birth family. I thought I had not choice and didn't say anything as I had tried that once before and didn't get heard, so what was the point? I just accepted it and got on with it. On paper I may be known as their surname but in my HEART I am always a Weldon.

I started piano lessons, which I found hard because I had small fingers and hands.

I had elocution lessons to help me speak proper but the teacher gave up in the end.

I had ballet lessons, which I did enjoy but I just did not have the body shape to take it any further.

Week by week, month by month, they attempted to mould me into what they wanted.

They had fostered me to help their daughter be less shy but it did not work. We were chalk and cheese you could say. They say opposites attract but do they always? We had nothing in common at all.

When Easter came around, we didn't get ash crosses on our foreheads but instead we got a daffodil and a chocolate Easter egg. We got quite a few, in fact, which I loved to share, while the daughter hid hers.

I got told off for things, which were routine in the homes but classed as rude in this family. Buttering my bread in the palm of my hand was bad, you must use a plate. I had to relearn myself into this foster family's way of life. It was a world away from my childhood roots. I just wanted to be me like the children's home had allowed me to be. They didn't try to change me. They created space for me and allowed all of me to unpack and not just my clothes.

It was like I was being erased and TRANSFORMED into a daughter that I did not feel in my heart. I can't lie or be fake so this is why I could only manage to practically pull it off like an actress. This was my role in my script now and this was my situation and circumstance.

The more I was changed, the more I HATED it there. I would write to the nun to tell her how unhappy I was. Her replies said it would get better.

I had months where I got on with it without any drama then there were months without any calm and only massive STORMS. I enjoyed watching television programs and films during the weekend. I would turn the television over when anyone wanted it changing because we weren't allowed to touch the television in the children's home, so it was a bit of a novelty for me.

There was so much I didn't know when I left the homes in every day life. I didn't know what a parking meter was as I had never seen one. It was like I had regressed to six years old or something as I asked many questions about life in the outside world. I was on catch up massively. I didn't know anything about music in the charts or what it was like to go clothes shopping in a shop, and not get them from a store cupboard.

I had a lot of firsts over the years with the foster family.

In one breath, family life was an adventure, but something was missing for me.

I just didn't feel like I BELONGED. I had my practical needs met. I had a roof over my head and my own small bedroom and food and clothes. What was missing for me was depth. I had been told that they wanted to foster me because their daughter was shy. I felt like I was a puppy to keep someone company. It was not about me but more about helping their daughter to grow. Love was missing for me in the sense they tried to change me which you could say is a form of love, but for me I felt like I wasn't accepted for me.

I just saw it like a job arrangement as they got paid for having me. I appreciated that they tried, we all did, but some things are more than just good ideas and intentions. They were a complete family and I was the odd one out. I felt like an INTRUDER.

I just didn't fit in.

Their sons were a lot older than me and at work, while their daughter was two years older than me and I noticed, as we got older, the daughter was treated differently than me.

I would run away from this foster home, as I hated my life. I would wait until they were out of the house or early evening when they were busy. I would climb out of a downstairs window if the coast was not clear for me to walk through the front door.

It did not take long for me to be found as everyone knew me in the community.

I would sit up in my room, listening to family life downstairs, not feeling a part of it, whether it was because I didn't want to or because I just felt that I couldn't see any of my roots in this family.

I missed the children's home as I fit in there and I had been allowed to be me.

This family felt like they where stripping me back so all I had left was a blank canvas, so they could paint me how they felt

I should be. I just wanted to have some space to grow from what I had already known. I didn't want to LOSE anymore of myself than I had already.

By the time I had reached my thirteenth birthday, my body had reached puberty.

I now had hormones to deal with and they were as ERRATIC as my life had been.

Nothing seemed plain sailing in my life, always a drama and ten times worse than it should be. PERSONALLY my life was catching up with me, not just my physical body. It felt like the walls were CLOSING in on me in my brain. I was SUFFOCATING myself.

It wasn't like when I was younger when I could distract myself from my life by using my imagination and laughing until my tummy hurt, not in pain but joy.

I enjoyed following fashion and music and putting on makeup. My close friends taught me what I didn't know about life being a teenager. The foster daughter noticed that I was ahead in puberty from her. Not my fault or hers. It is what it was, but this caused a subliminal shift between us, as I was more like the big sister in physical body just not in years.

MY FIRST LOVE

At fourteen years old I went ice- skating with a friend to an ice rink in Queensway. We used the central line to get there. My friend met a boy on the rink and wanted to meet up with him after ice-skating. This left me to pair up with his mate. It was lucky as I liked him and he liked me so this foursome worked out. I continued to see him every weekend and stay at his over the weekend too. I was in love. I had never felt anything like it. I was totally hooked on this love, as it was better than any of my previous experiences.

I lost my virginity with him, if you ignore my childhood experiences. I guess you could say I gave my consent, as it was my choice. At this moment I had blocked out my childhood and it was like it had not happened to me anyway.

So this is love, I thought. It certainly made me feel nice although I had been used to having a drink of alcohol beforehand. This helped me forget about the physical body and be numb to it; it wasn't so much the sexual act for me it was the love feeling that came with it. The actual act was not much fun and uncomfortable. It was having the CLOSENESS and undivided attention that I craved. I could not get enough of sex if this is what you unwrapped and got. As long as I had a drink beforehand, my brain and body was numb and I just craved extracting the love from the act.

I now thought sex was love and so any given opportunity I would be up for it. I didn't care. I had no self-respect as I wasn't worthy of love unless it came like this.

You use me and I use you, as long as you give me love I don't take the sexual act personally.

I thought I was happy finally and got everything I wanted. I loved staying at my boyfriend's house as they accepted me for me; they hadn't tried to change me. This gave me a change of scene to my foster home, something to compare family life with. The foster family was OK with me staying at my boyfriend's house as they knew his family would be at home.

I coped with the foster home the more space I had to myself. At fifteen years old, I went out with a friend from school. We decided to have a go on the boats on the lake. Holding a paddle each, we could not row and ended up going round in circles.

Two boys in another boat rowed over to help us and we ended up chatting and exchanging phone numbers.

I felt bad chatting to these boys when I had a boyfriend, but at the same time got lonely in the week as we only saw each other at weekends. My boyfriend had also got a Saturday job so this meant less time together. I decided to call him up when I got home to finish it with him, as the distance between us was too much. I had not had a chance for my emotions to catch up with me regarding this decision; I was too DISTRACTED with this new situation that I had not planned but found myself in.

My friend and I arranged to meet up with these local boys the following weekend.

We bought alcohol and drank it at the park. I had been used to drinking with my boyfriend and his family. These boys were not used to it and got very drunk. So we walked them home and had to explain what happened to his cross mother at the door. We didn't see them again after that. I think we had been a bad influence on them.

It had been a whirlwind week. My life had taken a massive turn of my own making.

The realization of splitting up with my boyfriend of a year hit me.

I was HEARTBROKEN and gutted; I had traded in my boyfriend for this week of nothing. No love. Nothing. Just an embarrassing mess. On one hand I wanted to forget it never happened but on the other I was reminded it had happened as I had no boyfriend. I just can't two-time and become close to someone while I am connected with another. If only I could have LIED about this week, then I would not be in this mess. Just my own conscience could not do it. I would not have been able to live with myself.

I was so beside myself with a broken heart that the only way I felt I could make this feel any better was to PUNISH myself. I sat in my bedroom and got my compass out of my pencil case.

With the sharp end I carved out his first initial of his name onto my arm. I didn't even feel the pain as no pain could override the HURT I felt inside; this was only skin- deep. I carved many letters into my arm. It gave me comfort that he had left his mark on me. I had in fact not lost him as I carried a mark of our love on my skin. Maybe this was how tattoos came about; always being able to see what has meaning for you. I just didn't have ink, I just had my own blood.

A few weeks later I had a telephone call with my ex-boyfriend. We both were missing each other. I said how sorry I was and what a huge mistake I had made. I explained about the travel distance between us and that I missed him during the week. We decided to make more time and see each other, so our relationship was back on track.

I was so thankful to have a second chance and to have my little hairy monster of my boyfriend back. I called him my little hairy monster because he had a hairy chest.

We continued to meet up and we spent the summer holidays together. We also went to a nightclub in London.

My fourteenth year leading into my fifteen was my best year ever, if you ignore the blip. I was happy and felt a grown up, going to pubs and clubs and doing what grown ups do.

On my way home one night I was handed a business card from a man as I walked out of the tube station. He said he was looking for models. I was in too much of a rush to stop and chat and so I just took the card from him. As I sat on the tube train I started to read the details on the card. A seed had been planted. I had never been noticed before, only ignored or abused or rejected. I suddenly felt more than I had been. I knew I was not tall like my dad's side of the family; I was short after my mum's side. I decided I would call the agency on the card the next day. I felt more CURIOUS than anything as to why I had been handed a card, as I wasn't good looking. I had been born with bad eyes and a squint, the effects of being premature.

A friendly lady answered the other end of the phone. I explained that I had been handed a card. The lady said we would need to see you to see how photogenic you are. I hadn't a clue what she meant, but my curiosity got the better of me and so I made an appointment for the following weekend.

I turned up and was told to take a seat while I waited for my turn to be seen.

I was then called in and a man told me to sit on a chair and to look at the camera in different positions. *Seems easy enough*, I thought while trying to hold my stomach in. The man said he would look at the pictures and be in touch.

A few days later I got a call from the agency and they said they wanted to take more photos and do a photo shoot so that I would have an album. I asked if the album would cost me anything and I was assured that it was free. I thought it sounded like a good deal. Just turn up with my clothes and I would get a free album out of it. I didn't have any nice pictures of myself, and it felt good to have a label as a model rather than ugly bastard; I was called a bastard, as it was a word in which to describe an orphan. I made an appointment for the following weekend.

I turned up with my clothes, excited to have attention even if it was through the lens of a camera.

I changed into different outfits and my swimming costume, which was quite revealing, my breasts where well developed for my age and I easily looked about eighteen, even though I wasn't even fifteen yet. I was naive in this situation and only saw what I wanted to see. I received my album and I was pleased with what I saw. I showed my album to my boyfriend who thought it looked professional. I was called by the agency and told that they wanted to take more pictures and over the weeks I was asked to reveal more of my flesh. The foster family didn't know what I was getting up to. They didn't ask and so I didn't tell them. I didn't feel like I could say NO as I wasn't asked if I wanted to do the shots, it was like I had signed up for it and had no choice. I didn't want to lose the feeling of feeling better about myself.

I just got on with it and did the poses, as I knew it would be over soon. I was feeling LESS COMFORTABLE and not enjoying being a model anymore, especially as I wasn't getting paid.

The last straw came after a photo shoot with a male model. He was naked and in a strange way this made me feel BETTER. I thought if he was doing it, it must not be that wrong or bad. As the male model left to go home, I was left with the photographer as he had offered to give me a lift to the station. All of a sudden he unzipped his trousers and pushed my head down onto his genitals.

I didn't know what to do. I couldn't exactly say NO- with his hand firmly on my head.

I just had to get on with it until he had finished relieving himself in my mouth.

I felt sick and gagged with his contents in my mouth as it felt like lumpy porridge.

He pulled his trousers up and zipped himself back up. Not a word was said on the way to the train station. I was in shock and put off of ever having my picture taken again.

I never went back and put the sorry experience behind me; it would be my secret and something I was not proud of. It made me realize that some parts of the modeling industry used the innocence of the young. I was happy to keep my album though as they were well presented tasteful pictures.

I alone would know the bigger story behind them.

One day I was in the garden at the vicarage sunbathing while the sun was out. The gardener came over and showed me a picture on a page that he had opened in the magazine and said that he thought it was me. I didn't really look at the image closely, I just recognized the ring on the hand, and knew it was me in the image. I never knew where the photos ended up as I had never asked and I never got paid either. I thought my payment was the photo album. I just pushed the magazine away and told him that it wasn't me. He never mentioned it again and I kept my distance. Talk about the skeleton's in my closet coming out to haunt me.

I just prayed that no one in the church would see what he had. Luckily they weren't too explicit in the sense that what you see is what you get and nothing much else.

My life so far certainly had not been dull with one trauma and drama after the other.

If this was what adult life was like in an adult world of MANIPULATION and self- gratification, I did not want to become an adult. I never wanted to lose my childlike spirit, I made sure that, I didn't get swallowed up by the seriousness of the adult ego. I achieved this by not taking myself seriously and making sure I could laugh my way through diversity and not take my experiences personally.

I had just started my last year at school and I loved how my first sexual relationship had made me feel in CONTROL rather than being controlled as a child. I could be whatever I wanted to be, not realizing that I was turning my head on my history of abuse to manipulate it so I didn't remember it. I had become experienced at distracting myself from myself.

One thing I could not distract myself from was seeing ghosts as it was called. Feeling the energy in my room would keep me awake at night. I would beg my foster family to share a room with them as it made me feel SCARED. I hadn't felt scared when it happened when I was seven years old because it had felt NORMAL.

What I had been told by adults made me feel scared, not the ghosts personally. It was the thoughts that had been put in my head about ghost stories. The name should have given it away: ghost stories. Fact or fiction? That was the question.

I was taken to the doctor about my sleep fears. I had sleep tests done and the doctor said I had epilepsy although I had never had a fit in my life. I was given tablets to control their diagnosis but after three months I took myself off of them as they made me feel ill. I never had a follow up or anything and it was like the hospital visit had never happened. I never mentioned ghosts again as I didn't want to be given tablets because of it.

I was angry that I wasn't understood or believed and just labeled as having an illness or that something must be wrong with me, just because I could see what others couldn't.

I already didn't trust adults as they had ruined my life in one way or the other. Kids that I met were more open and understanding toward me. I now buried being psychic along with my childhood past.

My social worker thought it was a good idea to do a history scrapbook of my childhood before I left the care system at eighteen years old. I could feel the RESISTANCE in me surfacing like a volcano each time it was mentioned. I somehow knew deep down that this was not going to be fun visiting my history. I knew the pain ran deep.

I felt ANGRY that my social worker had INVADED my space from myself. I was given a photo album of my family and as I looked through the album, it was like being introduced to my family for the first time. I was shown the death certificates of my mum and dad. I had a lot going on and a lot of information to take in which left me with more questions than answers. I found out that the man I had called uncle as a child was in fact my half-brother and he was twenty-nine years older than I. We shared the same dad but different mothers.

My half-sister had a daughter who was eighteen years older so my half- sister was old enough to be my mum. I also had another half-brother who lived on his own. We all had the same dad. My mum had three sons, two of whom where placed into care and the eldest I had met after my mum had died. I have never met her two sons who went on to be fostered and adopted.

Visiting my family for the first time since being a child was comforting in one way and painful in another. They were my blood - roots but yet total STRANGERS.

I wanted to ask my half-brother lots of questions but he wasn't really interested in talking about it too much as it was a long time ago for him. But for me it was new as if it had just happened. My social worker had opened up a can of worms.

I did not know how to process the new information and cope with what I had buried inside. All that surfaced for me was not specific details about my past but rather emotions and feelings that I had buried. As each situation and circumstance turned like a page in a book of my life, a buried feeling would get triggered and fire out of me like a gun, often with no warning.

I had trouble controlling myself. I felt like I was SPLIT in two. I had a NICE me and another side of me that was an EVIL angry me. I use the word evil, as that is what the church describes as bad people that have sinned. I had a belly full of sins, it didn't matter to me whether I had created the sin or if someone else had. I was carrying them in my belly so therefore I owned it.

I hated my past, my feelings, and my life.

I was entering a dark space, and if I thought it couldn't get any worse, it just did.

My boyfriend called me and finished it with me. I felt it was payback because I had finished it with him before and this felt like it was his male pride and ego talking.

To be honest, our relationship hadn't been the same after our blip. It was like a crossing out on a clean piece of paper. No matter how much you ignore it, it is still subliminally there.

I was really upset. Now I knew what it felt like to be FINISHED. I took it on the chin as they say, as he had gotten the payback. This made me feel better in some ways as I felt we were even. He would always be my first love, one I would never forget who I will have a special place in my heart, not in my tummy of past ACHES.

I kept in touch with him and we stayed friends. In the meantime, my life felt like it had a big VOID in it where he once was. I struggled at school but giggled my way through.

My best friend had problems with her family so I didn't feel like it was just me who had a sad life. My foster family were going away on holiday and I didn't want to go with them, so I was placed into another children's home locally for the three weeks. This children's home was only around the corner from my best friend.

We both started going out with two brothers. We both decided to run away. She would run away from her family and I would run away from the children's home. We got the central line train to a place called the Elephant and Castle Station, and met up with our boyfriends. We stayed at their house for a couple of nights. Then my boyfriend told us that the police were looking for us because I was a ward of court in the care system.

We didn't want to get our boyfriends family into trouble so we packed our bags and left. We caught a train and ended up walking and stayed low in the forest for one night, but we PANICKED when we saw car headlights. So we ran from there and caught a train to Queensbury station where my first boyfriend lived. It was the only area on the central line that I knew. We found the shops and decided to stay the night.

A couple of boys came over and one recognized me. It was my ex-boyfriend's friend. He stayed with us and I ended up kissing him because he was a comfort in a crisis.

I thought I was possibly pregnant at the time. My friend also thought she was pregnant. As it turned out, we both weren't.

Suddenly from nowhere three police cars with flashing lights sped toward us and stopped. My heart SANK as we had been caught. We were put into different police cars and taken to the police station. The police asked us lots of questions, and we explained that the boys had done nothing wrong and that they were just supporting us. My ex's friend's mum came to pick him up. I felt so bad as she had not been in the best of health. I said how sorry we were and how her son was just looking out for us.

The boys left and my friend and I were placed in a police cell.

We stayed there all night and had to be watched going to the toilet which was a hole in a wooden bench. I came on which confirmed I was not pregnant, but I could not tell the policewoman so my friend gave me some extra clothes out of her bag.

My friend's dad picked her up in the early hours of the morning, which left me sitting on a plastic blue mattress on the floor. I was told that I had to wait for a social worker to pick me up. I was scared because I didn't know what PUNISHMENT I would get next. The social worker came to pick me up to take me back to the children's home.

I was quiet the whole journey as I looked out of the back window of the car. The social worker told me that we were lucky, as the night before there had been a murder at the back of the shops where we had decided to stay.

If it had been a day earlier we may not be alive to tell the tale. I had caused myself so much distress because I was running away from myself.

I missed how sex had made me feel connected; it gave me a feeling like I was spaced out. I felt like nothing could touch me during sex as long as I had a drink first, a time out from feeling anything yet feeling free at the same time.

I felt connected to SPACE of nothing when I felt in love.

When I didn't feel in love or a connection, I would feel nothing toward sex. . Sex was just like holding hands. I didn't know what all the fuss was about.

I liked how drink made me feel FEARLESS and like an actress. I could be whatever was required of me as long as I got undivided attention. It made me feel special and important rather than WORTHLESS.

Sex was just like a sweet wrapper that I unwrapped to get what I really wanted.

That feeling of being wanted enough to have sex with, feeling special and having one on one attention. Being in that space with someone where no one or anything else mattered.

I loved the feeling of FLIRTING but this was not a guarantee that it would lead to sex.

Some situations I found myself in, I observed no feelings or EMOTIONAL attachment, it felt like sexual rebellion.

I took a lot of my emotional FRUSTRATIONS out on sex; it was nothing to do with my sex drive.

The staff I had met back at the children's home ended up being really nice. They wanted to know my reasons for running away and encouraged me to stay for a bit and to give them a chance.

I agreed and was thankful that my punishment had only been a chat.

That afternoon I met up with the other kids that I was sharing my room with.

They said that to fit in there you had to prove yourself.

I asked what I had to do.

One of the kids out of the group walked over to me and handed me a razor blade out of a box that they used to shave their legs.

I was handed the sharp blade and told to cut myself on my arm. I laughed to myself inside and thought is that it?

So I scraped the blade across my arm until it bled.

They then gave me an aerosol can and sprayed it into a cloth into the lid and got me to breathe it in.

I felt a little light- headed and that was it. A knock at the door put a stop to this situation.

Downstairs in the laundry room I bumped into a girl that recognized me from my first children's home.

She told me that she left because she was eighteen and no longer in the care system, but was staying there until she got a place of her own.

It was nice to meet someone that I had history with.

The two weeks went by and the foster family's son came to pick me up.

Obviously everyone knew that I had run away from the children's home and anything I did from here on was like living in a gold fish bowl.

My life growing up had some privacy that I kept secret and to myself.

Now my life had many voices with many opinions from other people.

I would get visits from my social worker to see how I was getting on. The family tree was scrapped because it was too DISTRESSING; I just wasn't ready.

I did my two-week work experience. One week I spent working in a hospital, the second week I worked with other classmates in a nursery.

I loved working in the hospital as I had always wanted to be a nurse and this touched on one of my passions.

I found out that the hospital would have taken me on but because of my age I was too young for insurance purposes so my dream of becoming a nurse was shattered, as I could not wait over two years.

I left school and enrolled at a local college to do a city and guilds community care course. It didn't start until September so I had the summer holidays to enjoy myself.

During the holidays I had a dream that I was back in the children's home and our home had met up with another children's home from Walthamstow. We all would meet up once a year. This dream made me think of the sister who was our head nun in our home. I woke up and looked at my clock and it said 5am. I suddenly felt an urgency to call her. I waited until it was 9am and called the convent at Basildon asking a nun who answered the phone if I could speak to her.

The nun replied saying that she was so sorry but the sister had died at 5am this morning. I explained who I was and the nun told me that sister had tried getting in touch but could not get hold of me, as she knew that she was passing soon. I had a smile on my face and thought to myself *she may not have been able to get in touch with me physically but her soul had found a way*. I was happy that I was able to go to her funeral, which I would not have known about if she hadn't told me herself about her own passing. The nuns gave me a photo album of my time in the children's home and a ring that sister had looked after for me. It was a gold signet ring my parents bought for me but it was too big for me to wear. Sister looked after it for me all these years. I really felt cared for by her, as she hadn't done me any harm. You could say we had quite a connection.

I did cry at her funeral but not sad tears but rather more mixed emotions.

She had known me the longest in my short life so far.

After the summer holidays, I started college and made some lovely friends in my class and from other classes too.

I met my closest friend who was used to people like me as her mum fostered kids.

Our class went away for a week, I cannot remember to where, but while we were there a girl in our class had afro type hair like back in the homes.

She showed me how to French plait hair.

I would often meet up with my closest friend that I had made and she would stay at my house and I would stay at hers.

In the meantime, I was not getting on with my foster family and it continued to be a rocky path.

I had a visit from my social worker and she dictated different verses of the legal facts of law having to do with kids in foster care, most importantly because I was a ward of court, so the system was my legal guardian.

I had to have their permission to stay anywhere like any parent.

I hated it and told her that I was more than an act out of the legal book.

My relationship with my social worker was strained and unsettled like my life.

It was not long until I would leave college.

My friend and I applied for a job in an old people's home around the corner from me.

We both passed our college courses and started work on the same day at the old people's home.

One day at her house I stated to her that I fancied her brother.

He had not long split up from his girlfriend.

I didn't know how he knew that I liked him, unless his sister had said something but the next day that I went round there he asked me out.

Things changed and shifted.

I changed jobs and started work at a different old people's home while my friend got a totally different job altogether.

I then started to go round her house more to see her brother who was then my boyfriend than to see her.

She also started going out with someone her brother knew.

My social worker then turned up to explain that I had to show my weekly pay slips, so that they could work out how much the foster family gets paid, and how much I have to pay towards my keep.

This seemed so unfair to me as their real daughter didn't have to pay anything.

I earned £45 a week and I had to give £10 towards my keep. It left me with £35 to pay for my weekly bus pass and toiletries and clothes.

I just didn't have much to socialize with; it felt like all work and general responsibility.

One weekend when my boyfriend's parents were away, his sister, my college friend turned up with a couple of adult videos in her hands.

My friend showed me the back of one of the videos and pointed out that my picture was on it.

Luckily it was nothing too bad, just a picture of me holding my breasts.

I was MORTIFIED as I had not told anyone about the modeling I had done a couple of years ago.

It was my past secret.

My past no matter how well I hid it from people always had a tendency to show up unannounced.

It would always put me on the spot; I GUESS we all have a trail of experiences, mine were like toilet paper that trailed out behind me as if tucked in my knickers.

Luckily that was the end of that and life continued on an even scale.

I found working in the old people's home triggered my memories of my past.

Turning up to work one particular day was nothing like the day before. There was a lady we called Doris. Now to get Doris to the bathroom to have a shower took a bit of imagination. Doris loved her handbag and didn't go anywhere without it.

So I quickly took her bag off her lap and this resulted in her chasing me down the corridor to the bathroom. Once safely inside the bathroom I would then give her the handbag back.

If I were on an early morning shift, I would get the first bus of the day at 5.30am. I would wake up more during the half hour journey to work. My shift would start at 6.30am, which gave me enough time to have some breakfast first.

I walked round the rooms waking up the old people and one morning I saw Doris already up sitting in her chair. I said, "Good morning, Doris" to which she replied a loud, "Fuck off!"

What a way to be greeted first thing, full of happy cheer.

Experiences in the old people's home were never dull.

It is quite amazing what old people get up to behind closed doors.

One time I was asked to wheel a man with no legs into the washroom for a bath. I had never seen anyone with no legs and felt a bit nervous. I was with another member of staff, as it would take us both to lift him into the harness. This gentleman was lovely and put my mind at rest straight away when he told me to wash his feet.

Obviously his feet were not there but he did tell me he could still feel them.

One lady had the same name as me and she had amazing stories to tell about what happened during the war, and how she had children with different fathers. I loved chatting with her.

I walked into her lounge expecting to see her one particular morning only to find an empty chair where she would normally sit.

I was shocked as she wasn't very old or frail or ill.

I asked another member of staff where this lady was and I was told that she had passed away in her sleep.

I was so shocked and didn't expect her to exit so soon as she seemed so young mentally.

A few weeks later while on my afternoon shift a staff member called for my help.

I walked into the bedroom and was told to open all the windows.

I asked why because it would soon be freezing in there.

Staff told me that this lady had just passed away and we needed to lay her out as it was called.

Seeing someone else dead triggered my memory of finding my mum dead, and it took me right back.

A flood of emotions hit me like a tsunami – I didn't know how to handle how I felt. I felt ANGRIER and angrier.

What made it feel worse the relationship with my boyfriend was very argumentative since we were both strong and stubborn people.

Seeing him that night ended in a big argument and I left his house via the back gate since it lead to the bus stop outside his house.

I felt ALONE as I stood at the bus stop at 11pm at night. Surely you would not let your girlfriend stand outside alone while you're warm inside.

He did. I was out of sight and out of mind.

I hated my life and I hated myself and didn't want to be here anymore.

I had often cried secretly on my own into the photo I held of my real parents telling them how shitty my life was, asking them why they left me behind and not taken me with them.

What parents would leave their only child between them home alone?

I had so many feelings and thoughts going through my mind that I was getting myself in a confused mess and nothing made sense to me.

I was at a very low and dark point in my life where death is all I had to look forward to at work.

I did not want to go back and face more of what I had personally buried years ago.

I went downstairs and walked into the kitchen. I opened the medicine cupboard and found a pot of Paracetamol tablets and took them up to my room.

I counted over twenty tablets and thought that should be more than enough to kill myself.

I took all twenty and lay down on my bed. I wasn't even scared to die, as it would be a relief.

Then the realization of what I had done hit me and I started to feel physically SCARED.

I suddenly didn't want to die anymore. It was as if something woke me up in my senses.

I walked downstairs and told the foster parents that I had taken a load of tablets.

They then took me in the car to the local hospital.

I heard a nurse say they could not find a pulse, but luckily I didn't need my stomach pumped and I just felt sick.

The hospital kept me in so I could recover and they transferred me to the psychiatric ward.

I knew I wasn't nuts or had a mental problem I was just hurting inside from a trauma, my feelings had not healed on the inside and that's not the same thing as a mental illness. After all, it was me who listened to myself and had my own back. I knew, what I was doing, I wasn't out of control.

My life felt out of control but it didn't mean that I was.

I met other young people on the ward. We all had a different BATTLE going on. One young girl was battling an eating disorder. This took me back when I was at school and my friend asked me why my mum had died. I replied that I didn't really know but most probably because she was a big fat lady.

While I was in the children's home at four years old I would often tell staff that I was fat, pinching at my skin and bones in the bath. Truth is, I was underweight but all I saw was fat not skin. This is the danger of subliminal messages, or of what kids overhear when adults are talking, selecting only the basic words that are repeated.

After about a week, the nurses and my social worker were satisfied that I wasn't going to harm myself.

I showed them that I had gotten over this experience and got a grip on my past and made extra effort to stop events triggering me.

I left my job at the old people's home, as I didn't feel this was helping me since it was far too DEPRESSING.

I needed a totally change of scenery.

I went and stayed with my real niece from my real family. I stayed with her for a week to get my head together.

It was nice to have a family member to talk to.

I shared with her my experiences about seeing dead people and she told me this gift was in our family and that my Nan on my dad's side had experiences too. I suddenly felt more relaxed about myself and not a FREAK after all.

She told me my family history and how I had been born premature and weighed 2 pounds, 3 ounces.

My parents had been on holiday and that my mum's waters had gone in the pub. MY dad turned up at my niece's house and they thought it was to wish her a happy birthday but instead shocked them that I had been born. They thought he was joking, as he was known for his sense of humor.

We arranged to meet up with my half brothers at the local pub.

I could not believe how much one of my half brothers looked exactly the same as my dad. It was like seeing my dad all over again and it was a bit of a HEAD FUCK.

They smoked so I bought them some cigarettes and my half brother told me that I was like my dad as he would do things like that.

I FELT PROUD that I had resembled my dad in some ways.

My niece showed me pictures of myself when I was a young baby.

She told me how my mum had mental illness and believed that she was blind and would wear dark glasses.

I would stay with her and my half sister so they could build me up.

When my parents died she told me how they wanted to look after me but social services would not allow it as they only lived in a bedsit.

My other half brother had three young kids of his own; so he could not have me live with them either.

My other half brother lived on his own, being a constant worrier he barely could look after himself.

I visited my half sister who had multiple sclerosis. She could not talk and could not move, only swallow. I did not know what to say but she seemed pleased to see me.

A few months later, my half sister exited the earth, died as it is called here.

With my wages, I made sure I bought everyone in my real family and those that I lived with in the foster family a Christmas present.

I was so proud that I had done so all on my own.

The following June, I had arranged to visit my half brother in his flat which meant I had to get two buses and I wasn't very confident about finding my way there.

I ended up cancelling the trip and he was upset because he had bought cheese for us to have for lunch. I did feel badly, as he had previously told me how we were both like gypsies moving from pillar to post.

A few weeks later my niece called me on the phone, to say that my half brother had died and exited earth from a sudden heart attack.

I felt even worse especially after they had gone to his flat to empty out his things. They had found lots of pieces of paper. He had written how much he had spent every day down to the last pence.

He had been such a worrier. I was upset and shocked, as he was only forty-five years old.

I was sad that my last memory with him was me making him upset and letting him down by not turning up.

I had found out how most of my family died young and forty-five seemed a ballpoint number, which went on to stick in my mind.

I managed to get a local job in a shoe shop on the high road, which meant I didn't have to start work at the crack of dawn.

It meant I could walk to work every day and this saved me so much money because I no longer needed to buy a weekly bus pass.

But this also meant my wages were re-evaluated with social services and it meant if I had more money, I had to pay more towards my keep.

So it worked out I wasn't really any better off.

With my first weeks wages I bought a new skirt that showed my legs as if looking through curtains.

I was proud of my new fashion item that I had paid for with my own wages.

A few weeks later I went to get this particular skirt out of my wardrobe to wear. I noticed it was missing from my wardrobe and I asked the foster mum where it had gone.

She sheepishly told me that they had disposed of it, and threw it away as they did not see this item of clothing appropriate.

I felt like my space had been VIOLATED. I felt like I had been robbed in a place where my personal belongings should be safe.

I was so angry and upset not just about them throwing it away but because it had been done behind my back.

I never trusted them after that.

A few weeks later I overheard the mum talking to her daughter, as she found out that her daughter had been having an affair with a married man.

They noticed I had overheard their conversation as I walked past them to the bathroom. The mum pulled me to one side and pointed her finger in my face while sternly threatening me not to mention what I heard, telling me that the vicar should never hear of it, as it would break his heart.

The way I was being told off, you would have thought that I had done something wrong. All I had done was innocently walk to the bathroom to have a bath. It was not like I had been deliberately snooping on their conversation, I just happened to find myself in the same space as them. I was angry and hurt that my life was displayed in a goldfish bowl for all to see, yet when it came to their daughter, it was HIDDEN even from close family members.

I didn't want to have to carry her secret on top of all mine from my past and I RESENTED them for bringing me into it.

I did keep her secret to myself and I am only writing about it now because it's the truth and the vicar has passed and exited the earth, so it's safe for me to do so.

I am letting go of secrets that do not belong to me.

I understand now looking back that, they where protecting the vicar and so this situation was out of love but it hadn't felt like it. To me, it felt like a THREAT. If they had said to me, "Please do not ever mention this to him, as it would upset him," that would have been a different story.

Why don't adults say how it is, rather than out of fear and distrust to DRAMATIZE a situation to manipulate in a way so they feel in control?

I just took it that I could not be trusted or even be given the chance to be trusted.

I just kept my distance from here on out.

I loved working in the shoe shop as an assistant manageress. What this meant is that I had a set of keys to the shop and would lock up when the manager wasn't around.

I was trusted enough to have a set of keys. To be TRUSTED by strangers meant a lot to me because I had not been trusted by many up until that time in my life.

My past had not gotten in the way of my job and staff at work only knew me as Dee not even Dorothy. I had decided to be known as Dee since it's less of a mouthful.

I got on well with everyone and enjoyed how we had a laugh even while working hard.

My next birthday would be my 17th and this meant I only had a year left in the care system and I would leave on my 18th birthday. Previously, my foster family had wanted to adopt me but I didn't want that. All I had left officially of my real family was my surname. I may have used their name at school but as soon as I had left I would use my official surname again.

When my social worker found out what they had done, she said they had no right to do that, as they were not my legal guardians.

It seemed that even my foster family didn't like playing by the rules set out by social services. I guess they were trying to avoid embarrassment or questions. In one breath they would say, "This is our foster daughter, Dorothy," and in another breath they would try and hide it. I felt like I was an example of a good deed to the congregation of the church. Feelings and emotions, where not faced and often swept under the carpet, and so the meaning behind an action would get lost.

Nothing made sense to me the more I analyzed the adult world around me.

Around this time I was getting fed up with the arguments in my relationship with my boyfriend.

I had decided that I didn't want to go out with him anymore.

One night he drove me home and as I got out of his car, I said that I didn't want to go out with him anymore. I really meant it. I had my back to his car and I would not look back. I just needed to get through my front door. Then I heard him say these words, "NOW THAT I HAVE GOT YOU OUT OF THE GUTTER, AND THAT YOU'RE ALRIGHT AND DON'T NEED ME ANYMORE!"

My heart sank. All I felt in that moment is that I OWED HIM. I didn't know what I owed him for. In my head I was thankful that someone would want to give the likes of me a chance and even go out with me. He gave me a chance and now I didn't want him anymore. I owed him is all I heard, and so I turned around and got back in his car with my head down.

I don't even know what was said next. All I knew is that I was still going out with him only because he had made me feel that I owed him. My heart was no longer in it. It was more like duty, like paying back your taxes.

The following weekend we met up with some of his friends after he had played football. We went back to his friend's nan and granddad's place. They lived in a mobile home. I was always an extravert and smiled the biggest smile so I guess you could say I always had a welcoming smile on my face.

When we decided to leave, his granddad said his goodbyes and he held my face and tried to give me a French kiss. I stood frozen like a deer staring at car headlights. I didn't understand what was happening. Did he know my abused past and thought it was ok to do that? It freaked me out and I kept all my feelings to myself.

A few months later, my niece told me that she was throwing a birthday party. She asked me if I would like to make it a joint birthday party seeing as our birthday was on the same day.

She would be turning thirty-five and I would be turning seventeen.

I agreed not really understanding what she meant, as I hadn't met her friends before.

I felt bad because I had not explained to my friends that it was a joint birthday. My niece's friends got me a card but my friends hadn't gotten my niece one. I just thought I was turning up to her birthday party.

I drank way too much that night. My niece enjoyed telling all her friends that I was her aunt although she was eighteen years older than me.

My real family were like east end cockney type people. They loved a drink and a smoke.

I got smashed to say the least and the ending to the night I cannot remember.

A month had gone past and suddenly my boyfriend said, "You have not had your period." I was naive and didn't keep track to be honest.

I wasn't surprised that he had noticed as I had always suffered with heavy periods, so much so that my doctor put me on the pill to regulate them at thirteen years old.

I would only have one week off a month not bleeding and bleed for three weeks out of the month.

My boyfriend suggested that I should have a pregnancy test. He drove me to a clinic where they did the tests. The test result came back negative. I didn't give it much thought; it was like I wasn't in the room and only my boyfriend was.

Another month went past and again my boyfriend brought up how I still had not had my period and that he thought I should get another test done. I told him I couldn't be pregnant as the last test said negative but my boyfriend ignored what I said and drove me to the clinic. The test was done and the nurse called us into the room to speak to us. She said that I was ten weeks pregnant. I was shocked and said, "How is this possible if the last test came back negative?" The nurse went on to say that we had two weeks in which to decide what we wanted to do.

A part of me was happy that I could actually fall pregnant and having a child is something I wanted since I was four years old.

I was also sad. My boyfriend told me that I was unable to keep the baby, because I was still in the care system and his mum fosters and would get into trouble.

I didn't want to get his mum in to trouble. I felt like my hands where tied behind my back because of situation and circumstance.

Counting the months back now I know what happened that drunken night of our joint birthday party.

I could not even tell anyone or my foster family and this made me feel angry.

The cost of the abortion would be £350, which was money we didn't have.

So we sold our record collections, which covered the cost.

I cried myself to sleep every night. I held my tummy while saying sorry to my belly for the decision that I felt I had no control over.

I felt evil since this is what the church says. I would be a murderer to add to all the labels I had already received.

Nothing would be as bad as this.

I felt every emotion.

I told my foster family that I would be staying the night at my boyfriend's house.

I told my manager at work so she could cover for me, as it would mean having a day off from work.

My boyfriend dropped me off at the clinic and told me he would be returning the following morning. I held a tiny teddy bear that I had bought for this baby.

The morning came and my boyfriend picked me up and he looked happy that the situation had been sorted.

I was DEVESTATED as it was not over for me.

I went up to my room angry that I was unable to share what had happened.

I walked to work taking pigeon steps. It was uncomfortable to walk.

I was angry with my boyfriend for not giving me any choice, only his option.

I didn't really care or feel much after this as I felt numb and on autopilot.

It was getting closer to my 18th birthday and I wondered what would happen to me once I left the care system.

I don't really even know how it came about but we decided to get engaged. It didn't feel like a love thing more something that you do. We had an engagement party and people I knew from the children's home came.

I had not seen them for years and this stirred up mixed feelings inside of me.

It all felt bittersweet. I didn't feel as happy on the inside as I looked on the outside. I was putting on a BRAVE face.

I was happy to be getting married, as you get your happily-ever-after when you get married. Well, that's what the message says in films that I had watched.

The following May after our joint birthday is when my baby would have been born.

The day came and no mention of it from my boyfriend, such an important date to me and not even a mention.

All I felt was ANGER toward him.

Our wedding was being organized by the foster parents, and we didn't have much say in them. We appreciated that most things where covered by everyone chipping in.

We managed to find our own place and with so much to arrange, I did not have time to feel the sadness deep inside. I was pleased to be leaving the care system and this foster home, so marriage was an escape from one situation into another.

Two weeks before the wedding I went for a drink with a friend to my local pub. As we sat and drank our drinks I poured my heart out, saying that I didn't want to get married.

I was relieved that I had told someone, although this didn't change my situation.

I could not get out of it now as everything had been arranged.

I felt like a COWARD for the second time, not able to say how I truly felt, as I could not upset so many people.

The morning of my wedding I found out that my husband-to-be had gone to work.

I thought, *What the fuck? Who goes to work on their wedding day?*

It didn't feel like a fairytale loving start to my wedding day, just another working day for my soon-to-be-husband.

We said our vows and got married.

We set off for our honeymoon near a seaside town.

We moved in to our one-bedroom house and married life began.

OVERVIEW

Looking back over those years, love taught me so much more than the romance that is portrayed in films or words of love written on a card given for Valentine's Day.

Romance, if built on shaky foundations of situation and circumstance, could sway and change as quickly as any mood.

You can have different levels and layers of love.

Love reminded me of Pass the Parcel. You never knew what you would unwrap next.

I worked out that no matter how much you tried to dress love up, it would always unwrap the truth even if years later.

You cannot hide behind love, as love always reveals how you feel on all levels.

I had not found my fairytale ending just yet. Maybe the next chapter of my life would not be so disappointing.

I always knew what I wanted from four years old, but what you want does not always match up with a partner.

My happily ever after was not a priority found in my new husband. He was my ESCAPE and it could have been anyone, as my life of situation and circumstance was still focused on survival.

Getting married was the next best thing compared to staying in the foster home as I had outgrown it. I didn't realize this until years later. For now I wanted to believe in romance like in the movies and placed my bets on a happily ever after and trusted romance was not dead like my life had been. I wanted to believe that the sadness in my life was finally over. I wanted to trust that marriage would be the answer to what I had been searching for—that magical feeling of love like in the films.

I wanted to feel in love and belong, a feeling that I had not personally experienced yet.

I was happy to feel more independent and on my own two feet.

No more social workers, no more being a ward of court and no more foster homes.

Becoming married meant I was now free like normal people.

A piece of paper that meant I was nothing like my past, I was now an individual adult like everyone else.

As the saying goes, I had made my bed and it was now time for me to lie in it.

Even our honeymoon was not a bed of roses; I had cystitis, an infection caused by not peeing straight after intercourse.

Then we met up with his family for the duration of our honeymoon.

This is not how I thought a romantic honeymoon should be.

It burst my bubble of romance, that's for sure.

CHAPTER FOUR

19-27 YEARS

I had a belated 19th birthday gift arrive that I would treasure forever.

Toward the end of August I found out that I was pregnant.

I was over the moon, as I didn't know if I would have been punished after what happened the year before with the abortion.

I had carried so much loss inside, and although this pregnancy did not replace what I had lost, it was a real comfort.

All I ever wanted since I was four years old was to have a real baby of my own and to have a family that I belonged to.

I had always felt like the BLACK SHEEP of the family, it didn't matter whose family I visited, it would not change me from being a black sheep.

I had only been married a month and now I had to tell everyone that I was pregnant. I did a couple of home pregnancy tests just to be sure, because last time it didn't show up until I was ten weeks.

I told my husband and I can't say I had the happiest of reactions.

This time he could not say I had to get rid of it, because I was no longer in care and so no one could get in trouble.

At first my foster family didn't believe me, which came as no surprise to me.

I showed them the pregnancy test and yet they still didn't believe me until I had it confirmed from the doctor. Maybe they just didn't believe me and preferred the confirmation of a doctor, as tests are not always accurate.

I made an appointment with the doctor and he confirmed what I knew.

I felt really HAPPY and very PROTECTIVE of my tummy.

I went to all the antenatal appointments and felt very SICK most of the nine months.

I even went to some of the antenatal appointments on my own, as my new husband didn't want to go.

I remember having a shower before my appointment and CRYING as I washed my growing bump. I felt so ALONE.

I watched as other women in the class had loving partners; I observed how they held them with so much pride.

My husband was just getting the hump with me for feeling sick and for deliberately falling pregnant.

I didn't know I had, as I thought that it was ok once you got married; I thought it came as part of the package.

Why wait anyway when it's expected once you get married?

I thought he would have felt the same way as me after we had already lost our first child.

I now realized he wasn't on the same page as me, and I was being punished for something we both had created. Surely if he didn't want one he should have made sure it didn't happen.

What a start to married life this was, something that should be such a happy experience was starting to feel more SAD than fun.

This was not my idea of happily ever after.

The bigger my tummy, grew the more he got impatient with me.

I would wake up in the night having to go to the toilet, which gave him the hump.

My due date was the 5th June 1987. Twelve days before my due date, my waters went very slowly.

I got admitted to my chosen hospital, as it had been 24 hours since my waters had gone without any contractions.

I met a few other women in the same situation as mine. I was getting impatient and just wanted to give birth now. I wasn't in any pain as I wasn't having any contractions at this point.

My husband visited me but stayed with me during the actual birth.

The nurses induced me and four hours later I had a healthy baby girl on the 26th May 1987.

I was a young new mum, three months off my 20th birthday.

I finally had my real baby at the foot of my hospital bed. It was worth all the sadness and the disappointment that I had caused during the nine months of pregnancy. At that point I didn't care if I was blamed for the rest of my days. Seeing my beautiful baby daughter made my life worth living for.

Not long after giving birth I wanted to have a pee, so I called a nurse over.

The nurse handed me a metal bed- pan and then closed the curtains around my bed.

I thought *What do I do with this?*

So I stood up on to the bed and held the metal pan between my legs to do a pee.

I thought nothing of it until I heard a nurse shout at me as she walked into the ward. "Mrs … what are you doing?"

I looked up and saw the nurse walking towards my bed as my head peered over the top of the curtain rails like I was a giraffe.

All the other new mums on the wards all looked in my direction and noticed my predicament,

The nurse told me to sit down and asked what on earth I was doing. I told her that I was trying to use the bedpan. She said, "You are supposed to sit on it not stand up!"

It all seemed a bit hit and miss if you asked me; I was totally clumsy with this gadget and instead asked the nurse if I could use a normal toilet. To my relief, she said I could but I did see the funny side. I must have looked a sight! A new mum having just given birth, standing up on her bed with her head poking up over the curtain pole. You could not make it up if you tried, it could only happen to me.

As I always say during adversity, YA GOTTA LAUGH AIN'T YA. It's certainly never dull in my life.

We lived in a small one-bedroom house but it was perfect. We didn't have much money but we got by.

I finally got my family that I had waited all my life for. At first we had enough room in our bedroom for her cot. In those early days we both helped feed and change our baby.

As our daughter grew we decided that we needed to move to a bigger house.

We sold our house and moved into a three-bedroomed house that was opposite from my husband's parents.

It was amazing to have so much more room, but we didn't have the furniture at first to fill it.

We got to know our neighbours who lived next door. They had a small child of their own.

I loved being a mum and was growing into the role as my child grew.

However, one particular day she threw herself on the floor during a tantrum in our kitchen being in the terrible twos. I felt at a loss to stop her tantrum so I left the kitchen and shut the door and stood on a chair so I could see her through the glass of the door. I saw her crying, but at that moment it was like I wasn't looking at my daughter but I was looking at myself. It didn't help that she looked like me when I was her age.

That image TRIGGERED me back to when I was two years old.

I ENJOYED for one second seeing her cry, because it was like I was looking at myself. I must have shocked myself at this revelation as it woke myself up out of this memory.

I thought to myself, *What are you doing?* Seconds had only gone by but it felt like minutes.

I got off the chair and opened the door and hugged my daughter and we both cried together in each other's arms.

This experience taught me how our history repeats itself.

I swore to myself that I would never allow my past to hurt my child and I would do everything in my power to protect my child from my history.

I had a big wake up call about how the past can be triggered when you least expect it.

I had zoned out and faced myself and felt how others had treated me at two years old and I was not going to let my daughter ever feel that again.

I felt awful and it is something that I would have to live with for the rest of my life. My daughter didn't know what happened from my side of the door, but I knew which was enough for me to get a grip of my past and make sure I held the reins.

I was thankful that it happened and I was thankful that in reality it only lasted seconds so no harm was done.

As I put her to bed that night after reading her a story, I stroked her head as she fell asleep.

I went downstairs and tidied up from the day, I put the kettle on to make a cup of coffee and sat down to watch the television.

The event of what happened kept replaying over and over in my mind.

I felt like such a BAD mum; I didn't want to be a bad mum like I had been a bad child. I wasn't a bad child, but that's what had been said to me and when you hear something enough, you start to believe it. I knew my heart was in the right place, I was just buried under a lot of hurt that I was carrying.

I went back upstairs and into where my daughter was sleeping.

I lay gently next to her on her bed careful not to wake her.

I held her gently saying how sorry I was about what happened today. The tears fell from my cheeks making her hair wet.

I kept telling her how much I loved her and promised her that I would try and be a better mummy tomorrow.

In that moment, all I could do was say sorry and tell her how much I loved her.

No words would ever erase how I felt that day, but in that moment it wasn't about how I felt, it was about my daughter. I didn't expect forgiveness for what I had done, just a chance to make amends.

I wanted my daughter to have everything that I didn't have growing up, a settled and loving family.

My life revolved around my daughter. I'll never forget when I first took her outside in her pram when she was ten days old.

You weren't allowed to take babies out before the ten days back then because of their immune systems.

I walked to the shops feeling so PROUD but at the same time so protective.

In the news that week a child had been taken and so this made me feel extra protective.

I held on to that pram like my life depended on it, my knuckles shone as I held the pram so tightly.

I admit people didn't think I would be a very good mum because of my past, I had been told this, years later.

It wasn't about proving them wrong and me right; I just wanted to love my child to the best of my ability, as this is all I had to offer.

I know I didn't have much experience about family life like other new parents. I didn't have my own parents to go on. I had not experienced a close, loving, emotionally nurturing family. It was just a practical arrangement.

I only had bad memories and so I didn't want my parenting skills mirroring that.

Around Christmas I found out that I was expecting our second child. We did talk about growing our family, as it was what you did back then.

I helped out a friend by looking after her son while she went to work. She paid me a donation of what she could afford

I didn't do things for money I did them because I cared, so the money was just a bonus but not my main reason.

As my friend picked up her child, she told me that her dad would be able to look after him from now on.

Her dad happened to live in the opposite row of houses at the back of our house on this housing estate.

One day he invited me round so our children could play together. I just got up about to leave when her dad pulled me on to his lap and started moving his legs under my legs. I froze for a moment, not knowing what to do but then I quickly got up and picked my daughter up and left the house.

This was the second time something had happened to me from the same family. The first being when his dad tried to kiss me.

I thought what is it about me that men feel they can treat me like that?

Why is it that adults take being innocently friendly as a sex signal?

How was I meant to behave around adults?

Just be emotionless and not smile or look at anyone in the face?

It seemed like I had an invisible label on my head saying Abuse me! Take advantage of me!

I was totally confused; I knew I was friendly in a chatty way as I had always been a talker. I was just innocently being me.

I didn't know talking in general was a come on.

The more I mixed with adults the more they confused me.

This man would often stare from his kitchen into my living room. Because the houses backed on to each other I felt like I had no privacy.

One day I had enough and I told my husband's mum and she came round and saw him staring into my lounge, she got up and stared right back and waved to him through the window. He never looked into my lounge after that. And I made sure I kept my distance.

Two men from the same family, my husband's friend's dad and his dad treating me like that? And I thought my life was fucked up.

The next few months flew by and before I knew it, it was my due date.

I woke up and started to make our bed.

As I made the bed I could feel something wet in my knickers; I went to the toilet and saw a pink jelly blob. It was called a show.

I started to get contractions and it wasn't long before they were a few minutes apart.

My husband drove me to the hospital, and his mum looked after our daughter. Once we arrived the nurse said after she had examined me that I was five centimeters dilated.

Two hours later I gave birth to another beautiful baby daughter.

I had only just gotten to our ward and my husband said he was going to play football.

I thought, *Seriously who does that?*

It's not like he played professional football for a job.

I was FUMING as I felt he was just not taking marriage and having babies seriously.

It's not like he had waited through a long labour; it was only a couple of hours out of his day.

I felt EMBARRASSED as the other mums on the ward had loving husbands by their side.

I had not forgiven him for working on our wedding day and now this. I felt the world should stop for the birth of your kids if there is no other emergency, and playing football was not an emergency in my book.

It just left a bitter taste in my mouth and I just lost all respect for him as I felt he was being very SELFISH. I didn't have the energy to moan at him. I just kept how I felt to MYSELF. I had carried our beautiful daughter for nine months and he finally gets a chance to meet her only to leave us for football.

It's not like he had responsibilities and taught it to other kids, this was a grown man just playing for pleasure.

Home life carried on. I focused on our children and my husband worked to provide for his family. We ate as a family and went food shopping together. Like most families, the kids came first. It wasn't all bad. We did have days out and arranged birthday parties for our children.

I'd had to give up being a waitress at our local pub on Sunday's where I also made starters for the menu during the week. Without my small wage coming in, the extra child benefit didn't cover it.

My husband made it clear that I should get out to work and so I agreed and did what was expected of me.

When my second daughter reached five weeks old, I felt I could go to work and I managed to get a job stacking shelves in a supermarket in the evenings.

I didn't bother waiting for my sixth week postnatal check up.

The hours I was given worked out great, as I could see to our children in the day and get them bathed and ready for bed, ready for when my husband got home to take over.

I didn't drive yet and so my husband gave me a lift to work.

I enjoyed working there and everyone was friendly.

I worked three nights a week. After my Friday night shift, I'd put my pen in my uniform and hang it in the wardrobe, ready for work on Sunday.

On a Saturday before work, we needed a pen to write a card. I knew I had one in my work uniform, so I went upstairs to get it.

It was not in my uniform pocket where I had last put it. I looked everywhere and even took everything out of the wardrobe, as I had known I had put it in the pocket the day before.

Sunday came and it was time for work, I still could not find my pen, searching through our junk draw in the kitchen. I found a broken plastic biro that still worked if I held the ink cartridge to stop it falling out of the plastic casing.

I went to work and when it was break time, some of us girls went to the toilet. I walked into the cubicle and as I went to pull up my uniform to pull down my knickers, a pen fell in front of me from above my head. I looked above to see if anyone was mucking about, but no one was there. I looked under the door to see if anyone had dropped it from outside the cubicle but again, no one was there.

I picked the pen up and put it in my pocket. It looked exactly like the one I had lost at home.

I asked everyone on the shop floor that night if anyone had lost a pen. No one had and so I went home with two pens, the old broken one and one that looked exactly like the one I had lost. It was like it had reappeared out of thin air.

Psychic phenomena maybe. What else could it be?

A few weeks later, my eldest child started playgroup. While she was there and while I was back at home, I decided to feed my six months old baby in her bouncer rather than the highchair.

I had just put a mouthful of food in her mouth and was waiting for her to eat it. I looked out of our patio doors at the garden and right before my eyes was the nun from the homes that had passed away, walking down my garden path. I could not see her actual feet touch the ground and it was hazy around the hemline of her uniform. As soon as I had realized that it was the nun, she disappeared.

I certainly wasn't expecting that to happen.

I guess she just wanted to let me know that she was ok, and so I would not forget that I could see dead people. I didn't see them as ghosts.

As a teenager I had tried to shut out all the psychic phenomena stuff and keep a lid on it. I just wanted to try and be physically human without that side of me getting in my way.

And now I didn't encourage it or try to connect with it; I just concentrated on being a mum and working to provide some money toward our household bills.

I had worked at the supermarket for three months and as much as I enjoyed it, I wanted to get a job closer to home.

It wasn't convenient with my husband having to pick me up so late at night so I got a waiting staff position, along with my friend, at a hotel just around the corner.

We both would be working three evenings a week, 6pm until 1130pm, or until all the work had been completed.

This worked out perfectly for me, as I had been used to working three days a week in my previous job.

I said I could start in one week's time, as I had to hand in my notice to my current employer.

We both decided to start work on the same date and in the meantime we were shown where to pick up our uniforms for our waitress positions.

The uniform was a smart black skirt with a white shirt and a full black apron and waistcoat with a bow tie.

I must admit I loved it as it made me feel part of an important TEAM. It was a lot better than my last uniform working at the supermarket. I had never seen such a uniform before. I thought it looked classy.

This job fit into my life perfectly and came at the right time, as it offered me more than just a job. It offered me a DISTRACTION from my loveless marriage.

Don't get me wrong; we both tried in our own ways and we were both committed to our practical arrangement but we just weren't emotionally on the same page.

We managed our day to day life of routine well and worked as a team and it benefited both of us, and our children to do so.

Each argument we had, highlighted the DISSAPOINTMENT that we felt, which created RESENTMENT towards each other.

He resented me for getting pregnant. I resented him for not giving me his heart and emotions, just his practical deeds, with his *I'm-here-aren't-I?* attitude.

I had two thorns in my side of hurt: the day we got married and the birth of my second child. To me, this was not love, it was rejection. His heart was not in it.

It was like we had a DUTY to be in our relationship and it made it feel like a JOB to do, rather than a loving exchange.

I had carried my childhood emotions in my tummy. I carried the thorns of my adult hurts inside my heart.

I may have been classed and labeled a lot of things but one thing the children's home taught me was to stick together and be loyal.

There, we had no need to lie and cheat one another. What we saw is what we got from each other and we faced the truth even if meant getting told off.

The more people that I met outside of the children's home, I found to be more complicated and not as easy to communicate with.

I didn't have physical humans in my life long enough to forge healthy relationships that would last a lifetime. I accepted that people came and went from my life and that nothing lasted for long, except the children that I gave birth to.

In the moment of each waking day all I could do was turn up and offer the best of my ability. I always gave hundred percent in any situation. I worked hard and made sure I had not just practical things covered but emotional ones too. I always put myself in other people's shoes and tried to not just view things from my own perspective

I wasn't ignorant and I had not forgotten where I had come from. Just because I was now married and had children, it didn't erase my past.

My foster family were of an era where children were seen and not heard, and your emotions where swept under the carpet. If there were issues, they didn't talk about them. They felt talking about them would be magnifying the situation.

In an ideal world no one argued or disagreed.

How do you avoid your feelings?

I knew I couldn't and that my conscience wouldn't allow me.

I felt not just my own feelings but also the feelings of people that I met.

Being psychic and a sensitive in some ways made me find out about life the hard way.

Physical people could meet each other and take one another at face value or only skin deep.

Being a sensitive meant that I saw past the flesh and bones; I could see and feel what people hid from one another. Deep down the truth and insecurities became BOLD for me that it was hard for me to ignore it. People may say they are OK when they don't feel it inside. I would not go with the OK answer alone as I picked up how they felt too. Having more to go on gave me a bigger picture on how someone was really feeling rather than just replying.

Inside my body I had lots of different pieces of my life stored, just waiting for me to piece together.

I also had many pieces that I carried that didn't belong to me, pieces that belonged to the people that I had met.

At that moment in my life, I was still in survival mode and helping my husband to keep our home above water so we didn't sink. That was the situation of my practical reality and it was the reality that I found myself in. My puzzle was going to have to wait to get pieced together.

As a mum, I chose to put my children first and anything about myself was farther down my list.

For years I would not make it up to the top of my own list, as there was always something or someone else that came first. This is true for most mothers, but as children grow this gives mothers more time to be at the top of their list.

Being brought up around religion it was drummed into me to think of others and forget about yourself and this is something that I found easy to do.

I thought by ignoring myself and always putting others first and focusing on their needs, that would make life HAPPY. I thought that if I could make others happy, then I would have a happy life. How wrong I had been.

I tried so hard to bury my self within myself. I tried to become a shell of myself and be a numb robot. I loved being a mum and it was the one thing I valued above myself.

I tried to just wake up and turn up and do my duty and jobs like everyone else did.

The truth in me would shout out, scream out, or speak out when I least expected it. With a past that is buried in time, events would trigger my past and bring it to the surface.

If I believed in something I would stand by what I believed. I could not pretend or go along with situations just to keep people happy. I had to have a connection with whatever I did in my life.

It was like I had another me inside of myself that I found hard to shut up and control. I found it was a side of me that felt stronger than the physical side of me that functioned on auto-pilot.

It was easy to just nod and smile in the right places of a conversation to be polite.

Life around me felt like a big stage where I met actors acting through their life and blagging through their lines, or making it up as they went along. There are many reasons why we may act our way through life, whether to save face or to escape.

I even felt people had MEMORIZED what to say next on cue but often didn't feel what they were saying.

The more I observed it going on in plain sight the more obvious it was and the more I didn't want to be part of it and brainwashed into thinking that this is truth. As an example it is easy to say you love someone, when in truth you do not, but it is easy to go along with it than to be honest as it would create a bigger change than going along with it.

I noticed how society teaches us to follow the main script then we create our lines to fit in to that script. We are taught to walk the straight and narrow, to not think outside the box and to follow the mainframe of what is set. Do not upset the apple cart and go with what is expected of you. At school I was not very good at English or languages and yet I still had to do them, although it was obvious I had my limitations.

I would not always conform and play the part and I would feel ISOLATED and judged.

I could see what was going on but was I the only one seeing the bigger picture?

This is the deep analyzing side of me.

I often got told off for being too deep or intense by members of the foster family and by those who crossed my path but I didn't see it that way. All I was trying to do was to make sense of the confusing way of life around me. It was confusing to me because what people said did not always match their actions.

It was like working out the puzzle of society.

I hated it there because of what I was observing and because I knew I had found myself in a dilemma. I could not fit in to this way of life set out by previous generations. I was told a saying: if you can't beat them then join them.

We are the majority. You are the minority. I was told this saying once when I had to confront the school about an issue and a school governor came to my house using this sentence as a threat.

Being a minority didn't bother me, what bothered me is how the way of life around me didn't match up with my truth.

I focused on what I felt comfortable with in life and that was the love I felt for my children.

It was amazing! My children didn't judge me. I could play with them and make up imaginary games.

I preferred how children played in life compared to the play-acting that adults performed.

I knew my truth and as long as I believed me, that was all that mattered. My truth was just a matter of always being honest, but it is surprising how people do not want to know the truth because it may cause change.

I was my own biggest critic and trust me, I was a hard task master and boss on myself.

I never let myself get away with anything. If I felt I had done wrong to others, I would own my own shit regardless of the punishment. If I messed up at school, I wouldn't gripe if I had to then write a hundred lines. If I messed up at home, my foster parents may ground me. I took the punishment without argument.

I would rather own my shit and get punished so I could live with myself.

Within myself was the only solid space that I called home, if I was not settled and comfortable then my life would not be either.

It started off as a work in progress. I started by building the foundations of my inner self by facing truth and always being honest with myself first and not denying or withholding the truth.

I could not lie for the life of me, I was hopeless at it; I was one of those people that got labeled, an open book.

I was constantly working on myself to be a better version than the labeled me. I did this by observing myself, I watched how I communicated with other people and thought of how I would like to be known as a person. I worked out my own depth and meaning, with morals and manners.

I could not stop or control what people saw in me. That's life.

I decided to up my hours at work; I managed to get five days a week rather than just three.

I had a busy life looking after two children and working every week day evening. It was lovely to have the weekends free, even though I didn't get much of a lie in.

My marriage with my husband felt like we just passed in the night hardly seeing each other, which suited me to be honest.

He was busy with his own life and would play football in his spare time.

I felt like a football widow.

Even on our wedding anniversary he took me to the football club.

I hated football as much as he loved it. I resented it as it felt like there were three of us in our relationship.

Over the months we had grown even further apart. We were emotionally separate yet living together. At first in our marriage we didn't let our differences get in the way of family life, but as the years passed, our differences grew too big to cover up.

I asked him if he would leave me, as it would be easier for him to leave me than it would for me to leave, considering we just weren't on the same page.

He said to me, "The only way that I would leave you is if you had an affair."

This sentence gave me a seed of thought, a way to end this marriage.

I believed what he had said otherwise what is the point in saying it?

A tall dark-haired man started work in our brasserie restaurant. He was friendly and chatty. It was nice to get some attention. A group of us from work decided to go out clubbing, and go back to a colleague's house for after drinks.

At the after drinks party the dark-haired man started flirting with me. This gave me the idea to seize this opportunity to get out of my marriage.

I ended up sleeping with him and decided that I would tell my husband the next day so that he would leave me.

I thought once won't hurt if it's enough for my husband to leave me.

The next day once the kids where tucked up in bed, I told my husband what had happened the night before with the dark-haired man.

I said, "Now you can leave me."

My husband replied that he wouldn't leave me. I was shocked and hurt as it wasn't the reply I had expected. He wasn't angry, he showed no emotion, it was all matter of fact and you would have thought we were talking about the weather. I said, "But you told me that you would if this happened."

My heart sank, as he didn't mean what he had said. What a head fuck.

Now I had done a bad thing, which would not have crossed my mind if he had not put the thought in my head in the first place. I saw this thought he had planted as a way out of my marriage. But I didn't think for one minute he didn't mean what he had said, because it was such an important thing to say. I stupidly believed him and so I ran with it and it backfired.

In the eyes of the church, I had done such a bad thing. This is what I had been told by the people at church when I lived with the vicar family.

I thought to myself, *Great. Add this to the long list of my evil deeds.*

I gave up after this experience. I never trusted a word he said again.

I knew I could never undo what had happened.

It wasn't an affair. It was a one- night -stand.

Now I had tarnished my marriage and my husband had something to hold over me. He would look a saint and I would look like an adulterer.

Life carried on with the divide between us more obvious than ever.

I did a late shift before Christmas and all the waiting staff decided to drink the dregs at the end of the shift as we were clearing up, rather than throwing it away.

Being a lightweight, I got drunk after mixing different drinks.

A member of staff called a cab and took me home and walked me to my front door.

I had puked all down my shirt. What a sight. How I didn't get the sack, I don't know.

Maybe it was down to the Christmas spirit.

I was put to bed by my husband and crashed out fast asleep.

The next morning I woke up not only with a heavy head, I also felt wet between my legs and I still had some of my work clothes on.

I asked my husband if he had sex with me last night.

He said, "No."

I said, "You LIAR! What is all this wet between my legs?" as I wiped myself with my hand to show him.

I was FUMING that he had taken advantage of me while I was drunk.

I didn't think he would do such a thing.

I knew that I was his wife and that it meant he could have sex with me whenever but surely not when I was drunk.

It's one thing making love with your wife. It's another thing raping them.

I called my close friend who I worked with at the hotel who also happened to be his cousin, and I told her what had happened.

My marriage was totally over for me after this and I just wanted to get out of the marriage and fast.

But I was in a battle with myself.

What I wanted didn't matter compared to what I wanted for my children.

I was in a loveless marriage but I loved my children more.

I had decided that I would wait until I was in my forties and I would leave him once our children were grown up.

I didn't want my children to be brought up in a broken home like my childhood.

I wanted them to have what I hadn't had.

So I buried how I felt deep down inside and continued with every day surface life.

I left the hotel and decided to work around the children so I could put them to bed at night.

One weekend my husband had a friend over and while they where chatting I could see smoke rings appear from my husband's face as he sat on our sofa.

It got my attention because none of us smoked, and these smoke rings were so thick and clear that even my husband noticed them. He just accepted the strange happenings that went on. Luckily he didn't witness much, so it was just random to him.

Luckily his friend was out of the room at the time.

Another time one of my children's musical toys started to play music although they had no batteries in it.

I was used to living with phenomenal happenings in our house, it did not freak me out. In fact, it amused me.

Around Christmas time, I had fallen pregnant with our third child, even though we had used the safe method. I had been told you could not get pregnant when you have your period.

I had morning sickness all day long and it was severe.

I was struggling looking after two children with being sick so much. I could not keep anything down.

My husband thought that I was making a fuss about nothing. After all, it's just morning sickness.

Each time he lacked understanding and support I hated him more.

I decided to go to the doctors to see if I could be given anything to make it more manageable.

While I was there I started to bleed.

My husband took me to the hospital and I had a scan to see what was going on.

The screen was turned away from me and it was at this point I knew something wasn't right.

I was 12 weeks pregnant and so I knew what it should look like on the screen.

It just looked like a mass of grapes.

The doctor saw me and explained that I had a molar pregnancy, which is where the placenta takes over the baby and it turns into a mass that looks like grapes.

I was told that I would need to have a D&C, which was essentially a scraping of my uterus.

A nurse handed me some leaflets about a molar pregnancy. I left the hospital feeling NUMB and with mixed emotions.

Looking at the leaflet on the journey home, it explained that a molar pregnancy grows very quickly which explained why I looked bigger than three months.

The increase in hormones is what causes sever morning sickness.

This alone made me feel better, that I had a reason for feeling so sick, and that my husband should not have moaned.

I was also relieved that the tests from the scrape came back benign.

But a few weeks later I still felt unwell. It didn't help that a lady at the school came up to me to congratulate me on my pregnancy as I still had a visible bump.

I felt EMBARRASSED and said, "No, I am not pregnant. I've just had a miscarriage." She apologized and we walked on our way, never to mention it ever again.

While the kids were at school, I went back to the doctors to see why I still didn't feel well and they did a blood test that confirmed that I still had a raised pregnancy hormone.

I had to be readmitted for another D&C. – The doctor on the ward explained to me that it only takes one cell to be left from the last scrape, which resulted in the cells growing rapidly again.

After the procedure I was told that I would need to have a blood test every two weeks.

The cancer research sent me a blood package in the post; I would have to take it to the hospital where they take your blood, as it would need to be spun. They would then give me the blood to post back to the cancer research.

It took eight months until I was told my hormones were back to normal.

I was so thankful and relieved to not have to keep having blood tests every two weeks.

It was explained to me that if I became pregnant again that I would need further blood tests after the pregnancy was confirmed and that I would need extra monitoring throughout the pregnancy with extra scans in case the cells reappeared.

During those eight months, life revolved around our children and working.

I worked various different jobs. One of the jobs was doing a nightshift lifting huge cabbages onto to a conveyor belt for making coleslaw but I only lasted a week, as the hours were not convenient.

I worked at the school as a dinner lady and looked after three children in the day for a friend going through some difficulties.

I picked other people's children up after school. Home life felt more like a crèche than a home.

The interest rates went up to 19% and we struggled to pay our bills.

We got into debt, which took us years to get out of. It felt like I only saw my husband on Friday's when we would do our big food shop together. Because I could not drive, I would do the small groceries during the day.

I decided to stay at a friend's house with my children for a weekend because I wanted to see if my husband would miss me or us.

My husband dropped us off at my friend's house.

I was sure this would work and that he would miss not seeing us all weekend.

I was excited when Sunday came to see if my plan had worked.

To my disappointment we had only just got through the front door with our bags, when my husband told me he was going out to play football.

I just thought if that if didn't work, nothing would.

He didn't miss us. I just felt like a single parent.

I was sad for my children. His family and my foster family didn't see what he was like behind closed doors.

They only saw what I was like in reaction to him.

I continued with my driving lessons and passed on my third test.

I stayed in touch with my driving instructor as he had seen the strained situation with my marriage. We ended up driving to Wales with my children. I wanted to stay at my friends and he drove us because I didn't feel confident.

My husband found out and drove to my friend's house where he punched my driving instructor square on the nose. I was just looking for a way out of my marriage and it only needed a kind and friendly person.

I went back home with our children while my driving instructor went back to his home. We never spoke again after that.

It didn't help that phenomena happenings started to increase.

One night as I fell asleep; I was woken by the sound of my name being called.

As I opened my eyes, I noticed that I wasn't in my double bed or even my bedroom. I was in a single bed and the room was basic with a chair next to my bed and a door opening opposite me.

As I looked at the open door, a lady walked through. I recognized her straight away. It was my friend's mum who had passed away when my second daughter was first born.

I was so happy to see her that I sat up in bed, quickly crossing my legs like an excited child.

I blurted out in my excitement, "You look well!"

She replied, "Thank you. Yes, I am."

Immediately I felt AWKWARD thinking to myself, I just told a dead person that they looked well?

She looked so elegant in a long, flowing skirt with a blue knitted tank top that looked handmade.

Her hair and makeup looked immaculate. I stared at her and said, "Your hair looks lovely."

She smiled and said, "I have just had it done."

I thought to myself they must have amazing hairdressers available once you pass. Ha!

She sat down on the end of the bed and we chatted for what seemed ages.

When it was time for her to leave, she got up and bent over to shake my hand to say goodbye. I was reluctant to take her hand in mine, as I knew she was dead and dead people's hands are cold.

But, I was polite and I reached out my hand to shake hers.

The WARMTH I felt from her hand was like nothing I had ever felt before.

She left me with my own thoughts as she said, "I have got to go now." She left the room as quietly as she had arrived.

The next morning, I called her daughter to tell her of her mums visit.

This brought much COMFORT to her daughter and said her clothing is something that she would wear.

I learnt that day that you can not die for the life of you. You may let go of your flesh body, but your soul is just as solid if not more so, than the flesh and certainly warmer.

My hand was warm for the rest of the day so she had certainly left her mark on me.

The summer holidays soon arrived and we went away for a family caravan holiday.

When we got home after the holiday I found out that I was pregnant. This explained why I felt so tired while we were away. I wanted my marriage to work, so we continued like any married couple, and physical needs were met. I guess you could say we practically loved each other but were not in love with each other. You just continue on with life hoping a miracle will happen, but that miracle never comes.

The surface of everyday life does not delete or cover up what is felt deep down inside forever.

We had to move because we could not afford where we were living.

The house we moved into needed a lot of work so we got the main children's rooms decorated and the lounge.

I felt a bit NERVOUS this time around after the molar pregnancy.

I wondered if the molar pregnancy was my punishment for having an abortion years ago.

I had extra checks and scans, which put my mind at rest.

The day before my due date, I invited some friends over for a meal.

They left quite late and I started to feel slightly odd but didn't think too much of it. That is, until my contractions came on quickly. We rushed to drop our children to his parents on the way to the hospital and we only just made it in time.

As we entered the lift to get to the ward, I felt like I wanted to push.

I had a baby girl half an hour later.

I was so happy and my husband didn't go to football this time, just home to bed.

I found it easier having three children. I found two took more of an adjustment.

I had my blood test from the cancer research, which came back normal.

Again they told me if I went on to have any further children that I would need another blood test.

I made a lovely friend with a neighbour down the road who had children similar in ages to mine.

I just wasn't happy in my marriage and it was taking a toll on my physical body.

I started to bleed heavily when I was on my period for weeks and months with only a few days off in between.

I had an appointment arranged to see a specialist as it had been going on for over a year.

The tension in my marriage was severe, so much so that I knew I could not wait until I was in my forties for us to split up.

It seemed no matter what I did, he would not leave me. As he made it clear that he would rather be in a loveless marriage than to face complete change. I felt like I was a prisoner in this marriage and under some kind of spell. If love hadn't meant so much to me then I could have carried on in a loveless marriage, and benefited from the practical security side of marriage.

The situation was making me ill.

I decided to set a date to leave him. I made arrangements to rent a house from a friend.

I arranged the date to be after my daughter's second birthday and I made sure our strained marriage didn't ruin my daughter's big day.

With my daughter's birthday out of the way I let my husband know what day I would be moving out with the children.

I got some suitcases and started to pack our things.

When my husband came home and saw me packing he told me to leave right away rather than when I had said.

I said, "The kids are in bed and I have not packed everything, and I haven't cleaned the house we are moving into."

He didn't care. He just wanted me out by the morning.

I cleaned our house so that he would not moan that I left him in a mess.

I then went to the rented house to clean it, so it was ready for us to move into. I finally got to bed in the early hours.

After a couple of hours sleep it was time to get my children up and ready for school.

Once I had dropped them off I started to pack what we needed in the car, my neighbour from down the road helped me. I needed the microwave for the children so I unplugged it from the socket and got it packed.

It took me all day to get packed and it was time for me to pick up my children from school.

They had activities after school so I wanted to make sure their routine stayed the same just from a different house was all.

My husband called me to say that I had unplugged the fridge and that it had defrosted.

I said I was sorry I hadn't realized that had happened as I had left in a rush.

I found it a struggle, as I had to wait six weeks for my benefits to come through.

I had sixty pound to live on a week. I managed to get a bridging loan to help me with my basic payments and for food.

Our children went to stay with their dad at the weekends.

I would never stop him from seeing them.

He made sure that his fridge was full with chocolate because I could not afford anything.

I felt he was trying to manipulate the situation so he looked better than me.

I ignored it, as I knew once I got settled my children would have biscuits like normal in the fridge too.

Those first six weeks were a shock. I had met my husband at sixteen years old and had entered through the doorway of adult life with him.

It didn't matter if we had loved or hated each other. He was all I had known so far. Although I hadn't been happy with him, I had been used to sharing the bills and the partnership that comes with managing a home.

Although I had been on my own all my life in the family sense, I had been used to sharing life with other adults.

To now find myself on my own with the responsibility of three children all under the ages of seven years old was massively OVERWHELMING.

I had no family for back up, my foster family and my husband's family both sided with him. They did not know what he was like. They only saw me as the problem, and I took responsibility for my part of our problems and situation.

I had no choice but to leave my husband as my health had pushed me to it.

The funny thing is as soon as I had left him; my periods went back to normal straight away. The stress of the marriage had taken its toll on my body and even my body told me enough was enough.

It was the scariest and hardest decision I have ever had to make.

It is something I wanted to avoid and wait until I was in my forties when the children were grownups themselves.

I was SAD inside. I never wanted my children to have the hard childhood that I had.

I wanted them to have a secure upbringing with two parents living under the same roof.

I would have given up everything for them if it meant they could have a normal family life, but my health put a stop to that.

It was like a double -edged sword. I was personally happy to be getting out of a loveless marriage with no respect. But on the other hand, I was grieving the family unit I wanted not only for my children but for myself too.

I received a letter in the post from my husband's mum, as if I hadn't had enough on my plate to deal with.

It was not a friendly letter and a bit threatening saying I had better let her son see his children.

I was shocked as I thought she knew me better than that.

I may have left her son taking our children with me, but I would never stop him from seeing them ever.

I was hurt at receiving the letter, as I had known his family for eleven years and just felt that everyone was AGAINST me.

They didn't know the whole story, only the bits they had observed. It would have been like observing a film without any sound or without subtitles.

You come to your own conclusions.

I put the letter away, and decided that I had now made my bed I have to lie in it and get on with it. There was no going back.

It wasn't like I had come to this decision quickly. It had taken me years.

It's not like we had a heated argument and I left out of anger.

I calmly packed my bags and communicated with my husband the best I could under the circumstances.

A few weeks later once my money had come through, I was able to budget and manage my weekly bills.

I knew our living conditions were not ideal.

Renting a friend's house while they were away on tour meant all their own belongings were still in the house.

This meant we only had one bedroom between the four of us.

My priority at that time wasn't luxury but of having a roof over our heads and making sure we were all together and not split up.

The summer months were soon upon us so everything we now faced in this new chapter of our lives was a first.

Everything felt NEW and UNFAMILIAR.

I had to get used to carrying everything on my own shoulders.

My ex-husband came round to give me a birthday gift and to talk about money.

He asked me how much I wanted a week for the children.

I said forty-pounds as I didn't want to be greedy and leave him short. I wanted to be fair as he had a life too.

He agreed and said he would give me what I asked.

A few days later he called me to ask if he could have a chat with me.

I let him in and he asked me if there was any chance of us getting back together.

This time I said no.

This time I didn't feel that I owed him to stay with him.

He left and that was that.

Leaving him I can honestly say I never looked back.

A couple of months later he met a woman from the football club that he belonged to.

She had a couple of children of her own.

I had started casually going out with a man my friend knew, but this only lasted a couple of months.

As much as our life was hectic, our routine stayed the same through this new chapter.

The only thing that had changed was my children lived with me and they saw their dad at weekends.

Once he met his new girlfriend the arrangements changed.

He now wanted to see them every other weekend.

His choice.

He started to get more hostile and wanted to make sure the money he gave me went to the children and not me.

He told me that our children would grow up to hate me. I believed every word he said. I believed him because of my unsettled upbringing. He had come from a secure background and I had not and I thought he knew something I didn't know. That one sentence I carried in my heart like a thorn in my side.

He was right, as I was from a broken home life and he was not. He had more to offer our children financially. All I could give them was my love.

He wanted me to produce receipts to prove his money went on the children and not me.

I said, "I cannot give you a receipt for everything. This is ridiculous."

So he chose to no longer give me cash and gave me a cheque instead. Then he stopped giving it weekly and it would be every two weeks when he saw the children.

I felt like he didn't realize that I relied on the forty pound he gave me, as he made receiving it so difficult.

Had he forgotten how expensive children are? Forty pound is a little over thirteen pound each child.

When he asked me at the time of us splitting up, I was unable to calculate or put a price on our children. At the time all I could think about was being fair to him, as I didn't want to make his life more difficult. I did not know how much I would need for my children, as I didn't know how I would manage my money yet.

It was all still too new and fresh.

I missed being married and the security that being married brought financially.

Within two weeks of my ex-husband meeting his girlfriend, he wanted our children to stay over at her house and share a bed with her children who were complete strangers to them.

I didn't feel this was fair and that he should at least introduce them before playing happy family. We may have had a clean divorce but we did not always see eye to eye.

We had only been split up six months and it felt all too soon for my children.

He didn't agree, obviously, and so the divide in our parenting practices became more apparent.

We were not on the same page when it came to the feelings of our children. All he could think about was what he wanted.

All he could say was that he had his own life now.

I knew I would not be able to rely on the forty pound that he should give me regularly and I knew I had to find a job to make ends meet.

And so the next chapter of my life would begin with me standing on my own two feet.

OVERVIEW

Looking back over these years, my life was transitioning from self-survival to sharing survival with my children.

It didn't matter how others judged me or labeled me. My priority was keeping my children in a safe and nurturing space.

I still carried the love balloon from my dad. I believed in love and no matter what bad experiences I had so far with love, there was no way I was giving up on IT.

I felt like the woman in the film Pretty Woman. I wanted the fairy tale like in the films.

I knew that my life was an ugly mess.

This didn't stop me from trusting in love. It wasn't love's fault that I had experienced what I had so far. It was how love had been managed and handled.

Ever since I was a child I had felt like I had a missing piece in my life, and my relationships did not fill this gaping hole.

I may not have found the love of my life yet, but my marriage gave me three special gifts – these gifts I would treasure throughout my lifetime.

If I had only met my husband in exchange for my children then all the pain and hurt was worth it.

I would not give up on my children for anything. I would rather be poor and have my children than rich without them.

Don't get me wrong being married was a more acceptable label in society than being in the care system.

I now had the label of a single mother, which had a bad reputation of damaged goods of a different kind back in the 90's.

My children came home after seeing their dad and they started to ask me awkward questions.

I knew there was no option to lie, so I told them the truth no matter how young they were but I told them the whole truth of why things happened the way they did as there is always a meaning behind things.

I already knew my husband had told me my children would grow up to hate me, and I thought this is where it starts once they know my TRUTH.

I was honest and owned my life and all its gory details.

It was one of the hardest things I had to do, owning up to not being perfect for my children.

I had flaws and inadequacies.

The thing is my children respected the truth and if anything it cemented the bond that we shared.

Honesty is the best policy. I was told by my foster family to not be honest with children but I knew in my heart they would be always old enough to face truth, as truth does not have an age limit.

I was relieved that no matter how ugly it got and how many low punches were taken, I felt confident that my girls would not be manipulated.

Sometimes our girls would try to play us against each other.

It would not work with me.

Once one of my daughters gloated about what her dad had given her. It was sixty pounds for her birthday.

I never gave my children cash as I got them presents to unwrap.

She started to gloat and not appreciate what she had in general no matter who had given it to her.

I said, "OK, if that's how you want to be, I want you to bag everything up that I have ever bought you. I mean everything."

What she was left with in her bedroom was sixty pounds and a few things that her dad had gotten her.

She was screaming and crying about how unfair I was.

I then told her, "You do not play your parents against each other. What happens in this house is down to me, what happens at your dad's house is down to him."

Two days went by and my daughter fully regretted what she had done.

We sat down and had a chat and a cuddle, she decided she wanted all her things back in her room and from then on appreciated what both parents bought her no matter how different it was.

I explained to her that I would always give her my best and that is all I could do.

I would always keep it real, which is why I would not entertain manipulation or mind games.

I also affirmed that I may be older than her, but I am not perfect and will make mistakes. I didn't learn how to be a parent and I was only following my heart as a guide.

Each day is new for all of us. All we can do is support one another as we face each day.

We were not scared to be ourselves even in anger and upset.

I was happy being divorced and glad to be getting my maiden name back, a name I had not had a chance to use since I left the children's home. By having my real surname again, Weldon, a piece of my history and link with my dad, made me feel like I BELONGED to him once again.

It felt like my life was on REPEAT; repeating similar labels just with a different scene.

I realized that you can live with people for many years and yet they do not really know you.

I understood that as long as I knew myself and listened to my conscience I would get through each hurdle that I would face.

After my marriage came to an end, I faced life with my children on my own. This was no different than my childhood growing up.

I still hadn't faced myself yet or found my own self-love or self-worth. I hadn't had a chance because I had responsibilities that came first.

What I took from this experience is how much I was in love with my children and I thank this chapter of my life for experiencing the unconditional love that I felt being a mother.

I now knew that I had a lot of love to give. Being open to love, I could equally take a lot of shit too.

I had the strength to face this not just for myself but for the love that I have for my children.

I may just be a single mother to other people but to me I was a mother who wanted to give my daughters all of me to the very best of my ability.

I was a learner at being a mummy and as my children grew, I grew with them.

I created a loving home. I had to start from scratch and make it a safe place where they were accepted just for being themselves.

My three children were different and had different needs. So I would follow their lead and give them the love they each individually needed while treating them the same. It helped that they were all girls.

Love had expanded from my self and now I was sharing love with my own family. It was not the norm of 2.4 children. We were 1.3 but together we had everything we needed.

Life was no longer about me. It was now all about my girls. They gave me a reason to get up every morning.

CHAPTER FIVE

28-35 YEARS

While at the school gates, I got talking to another mum about how I needed to find a job. She said that she was looking for someone to help with a sandwich round business she had just set up.

I said I would do it and the following weekend I went to her house so she could go through the job details with me.

It was an early start leaving at 7.30am each morning.

I didn't know how I would work around this, as I had no one to take my children to school.

Another friend I knew at the school had one child and so I asked her if she would take my children to school in exchange for me cleaning her house because I would not be able to afford to pay her.

I was so THANKFUL that she agreed.

This arrangement worked out for both of us.

My friend invited me round for a dinner party that she was having the following weekend.

I turned up with a bottle of wine and enjoyed socializing with these adults. They were so easy to get on with.

You know when you just meet some people and you feel like you have known them all your life?

Well, one of them started to share with me the problems that she was having in her marriage.

I felt for her and said how SORRY I was that she was going through that.

She loved her husband very much and would do anything for him.

I started to clean her house too in exchange for her having my children while I worked.

One day after cleaning her house she asked me if I would do her a favor, a favor she had asked her other friend but they had declined.

She asked me if I would partake in a threesome to spice up her marriage for her husband.

I had never had a threesome before and so I had no idea what a threesome entailed.

I felt really sorry for her and felt like I OWED her. I always felt like I owed people especially as she kindly accepted looking after my children without getting paid. I would not have been able to work without her help.

I agreed to do this one thing to help her marriage and we arranged to meet during the day the following week while the children were at school.

Luckily, we had a drink and I zoned out like I did as a teenager as she basically just wanted to watch her husband have sex with me.

I promptly left after the experience and we never repeated it or spoke about it after that.

Life carried on as normal as if nothing had happened.

In the meantime, my divorce came through and my ex husband stayed more at his girlfriend's house rather than at our ONCE marital home.

With Christmas soon upon us, we had agreed that I would have our girls during the day and he would pick them up in the evening and have them overnight so they could see the rest of his family on Boxing Day.

We had a lovely traditional Christmas with a full roast dinner and all the trimmings.

At 6pm my ex-husband came to pick them up and I waved goodbye. I told them how much I loved them and to have a FUN time with Daddy.

I now faced Christmas evening all alone.

It was the most surreal moment of silence.

They say silence is deadly because it certainly felt like it.

I sat on the sofa looking round at their opened presents from Father Christmas and the sweets on the side that I bought for them, so they had like a pick n mix sweet shop.

It made me feel like half of me was MISSING while they were not with me.

I had been used to always being around my children every day unless I had been at work. I had already felt like a single mum while I was married but this felt like one of my limbs had been SEVERED.

I had no choice but to accept the silence and situation that I was in. It reminded me of the SILENCE I felt when I found my mum dead at Christmastime all those years ago.

Luckily, in this situation, I knew my children would be back in a couple of days.

So I went to bed early so the next day would arrive more quickly.

I got the house all cleaned and tidy and ready for when the children would arrive back home.

When my children came home they told me all about their time at their dad's. My eldest daughter told me how her dad's sister had cut my face out of all the photos they had of us.

I was so HURT that my daughter had noticed that. I thought, *How could she be so cruel when I had supported her when she got pregnant on holiday?* I was the first person that she turned to and I held her hand as she told her mum.

I am so protective of my children. I thought, *You can hate me and hurt me to my face or behind my back, but don't do this to my children. They can't help that I am their mum.*

I don't think his sister ever knew that I knew what she had done but it's something I have never forgiven her for. I just cuddled my daughter and explained that they were angry with Mummy for not being with her dad. I said , "Don't worry it is just a photo, just a piece of paper. I am still your mum and your dad is still your dad."

The festive season soon passed and it was time to get my girls ready to go back to school.

I was glad to get my first Christmas on my own out of the way.

Just after my youngest daughters third birthday I received a letter from my friend who I was renting the house from.

The letter said that he was coming home from tour and would need his house back.

I now had to find a new roof for over our heads.

I didn't want to end up in a half-way house as my children had been through enough already. I wanted change to be minimal for them.

I looked through the local gazette to see if any rentals where available.

As I looked through, a mobile home for sale caught my eye. It was being sold for six thousand pounds.

I had a light bulb moment. I wanted to go and look at it.

I went with my friend from the school and looked around the site, which also had a shop on the land.

The mobile home had three bedrooms and was plenty big enough for the four of us. After all, we had been sharing a double bed and living out of our suitcases all these months.

The lady that showed me round was a parent with one child and was moving into a property with her boyfriend.

I was concerned with how I'd be able to save six thousand pounds when my wage was so small from the sandwich round.

I knew my ex-husband would not help me as he hadn't even offered.

I decided to make an appointment with my bank manager since I had been banking with this bank since I was sixteen years old.

I explained my situation and asked if I could apply for a loan so I could put a roof over my children's heads.

I don't know how I got accepted, because on paper I should have not been accepted, but miracles do happen and I got my six thousand pound loan.

Some people would say it was pure luck or being in the right place at the right time. I would say it was alignment and perfect timing because I knew what I wanted.

I bought the mobile home and a few weeks later we packed up our suitcases to move in.

It was our first real home of our own. I had to get use to buying bottled gas for the cooker and the heating.

It was old but we made it home best we could.

We all actually enjoyed it as it gave my girls the freedom and space to ride their bikes and play outside freely.

It was like a little community on this site; my girls would walk up to the top of the park site and buy things from the shop.

They had events on site where they got to dress up in fancy costumes. I made my eldest daughter's face into a flower, and my second daughter I made into a kite and my youngest daughter became the tin man from The Wizard of Oz.

I was pleased with their costumes although my youngest CRIED while wearing hers but she soon CHEERED up when as she came in first for the contest and won first prize.

On my sandwich round at work I met a man who seemed nice. I was missing being married and although I had been on my own without a boyfriend for only five months, I still missed that security of sharing life with someone.

Maybe it was because I had been brought up in institutions and marriage is classed as one.

I introduced this man to my children and they got on well.

He started to come round more and stayed over occasionally too.

In the meantime, my ex-husband had moved in properly with his girlfriend.

She behaved like she was jealous of my girls and of me, because she had nothing to do with her ex-husband and he had nothing to do with their children.

I felt because of this, my ex-husband seeing his children didn't sit well with her.

I felt she would have preferred to have him all to herself without us in the picture.

Not long after he had moved in, they had got engaged.

I was genuinely happy for them both.

To me it finalized everything and totally underlined it with no going back.

I bought them a card and wrote some HEARTFELT words inside but she did not take too kindly to the card at all.

I then knew there would be no bridges in this situation, only a divide.

I knew my place and I knew to keep my distance and take her at face value.

While my children went to stay with them every other weekend, I knew whatever happened at his house was out of my hands.

I received a letter from the landowner of where my mobile home was sited.

It stated the site rules it explained that any mobile home older than twelve years had to be upgraded to remain on the site.

Admittedly, mine had a bit of a damp problem, which didn't help my weak lungs.

I went to the council to see if there was any help since my name had been on the waiting list for years.

A lady from the housing department said that I would be at the top of the housing waiting list but that a mobile home was not classed as a home.

In the meantime, I still had to sort out the mobile home and was still paying the loan for it. If I couldn't sell it, I knew that I would not be able to pay the loan off.

A friend was willing to buy it from me and put a new roof on it.

I wrote a letter to the site manager to explain this but this request was declined because the mobile home was still too old.

The only way forward was to remove this mobile home and put a new one in its place.

I didn't have the money to do that.

Luckily, I was offered a three bedroom flat by the council.

I got the keys and showed my girls around the flat.

We where all so EXCITED as it had a lovely sized garden and was on the ground floor.

Six weeks later we moved in.

Our first solid home without any damp, with my money, and I could only afford one home not two.

I was stuck with a mobile home the site manager would not let me sell. I was in catch twenty-two.

I decided the only option moving forward, although it seemed extreme, was to go bankrupt.

I would not be able to afford the loan on top of paying for the flat.

So I went bankrupt. I felt relief on one hand to have a fresh start, but had a label of being BANKRUPT that would stay with me for the next six years.

I did think to myself, *Well, I'll just add it to my list with all the other labels that I had acquired in my life!*

I was no longer able to keep my sandwich round job because I had moved to a different area which also meant my children moved schools.

I lost touch with the friends I had from the old school, as life goes on and moves on.

My boyfriend moved in with us and we decided to get married and set the date for a couple of months later. This was a total rebound relationship with a man who meant well until responsibilities made life too much.

Talk about rushed, but I didn't want to give up on marriage; I wanted to believe in love so I was open to giving it a go.

My second husband now knew about my history and told me that he had a friend who worked in the funeral business.

He asked his mate to see if he could find out about the death of my parents.

As luck would have it, not only did he find out information about their funeral arrangements, he actually found the urn with my mother's ashes.

She was still at the funeral parlor! No one in my family had picked her ashes up after her funeral, not even her own children!

This reflected the LOVE LOSS between her and my dad's children, and even her own.

My mum may have been an outcast pretty much like how I have been but she was still my mum and my dad had loved her, a love it seems only he would understand and one he took to his grave.

I picked up my mum's ashes. It felt a STRANGE way of being reunited with my mum in death yet again.

I kept my mum's ashes for a few weeks and put her urn in the lounge.

I opened up her urn up to see what, her ashes looked like because I was curious.

Her ashes looked grey and white in colour and once I had a look, I questioned why would I be HOLDING on to them if she's, not here anymore.

I drove to where my dad had been buried and asked the man who worked there if he would mind putting my mum with my dad.

He said he didn't mind and would do so. I handed my mum's ashes over to him and trusted his word that he would put her with my dad.

I never went back again after that as I felt my mum would be at PEACE now.

The funeral director said that my mum's ashes had been there over twenty-two years, the longest they had ever stored someone's ashes and was quite SAD to see her go, as she had become part of the place.

I was thankful that my mum had not been left behind. Situations in my life had a synchronistic way of making sure that what crossed my path was what I needed. With my past left open like an open grave, being reunited with my mum gave me the opportunity of finishing her burial.

I may have been closer to my dad more than my mum. Because of grief, I BLANKED her out of my life.

My soul knew that in the physical there is unfinished business, which continued from where we left off.

Finding her ashes may have been a final chapter in my mum's physical life. It was a new chapter for me opening up. I just didn't know it yet.

I half felt bad for letting go of my mum when I had a chance to hold on to her even if it was only with her ashes but I knew holding onto the past does not open doors for the future.

It was out of love for my parents and for the love they shared together and that was my reason and meaning behind letting her go.

My second marriage lasted nine months. His heart was in the right place but the strain of paying all the bills became too much for him.

We argued and he lashed out. I told him to leave, which he did and he never came back. I felt that night had opened a door for him and he walked on through.

I was THANKFUL for the short time we shared together. If I had not met him I would not have been reunited with my mum.

Meeting him gave me a piece of my life puzzle back. I was the main backbone to my children's stability. As long as I kept their lives the same and secure, relationships not working had less of an impact.

I had to now start all over and apply for benefits yet again to pay my bills.

My life just seemed to constantly be on a short fuse and nothing stayed or lasted long in my life.

I sat outside in the fresh spring air with my head in my hands, feeling half- numb from the last night's event.

I was married one minute and again single the next. My life changing overnight seemed my normal pattern.

I heard a knock at the door and it was a man from the local council who had come to change my back gate.

I had completely forgotten that this had been arranged.

Last nights drama had completely distracted me.

I opened the door to a chatty dark-haired man full of energy.

I apologized for the state of me. I don't normally spill the beans about myself but he made me feel COMFORTABLE.

I told him how I had split up from my husband the night before.

It didn't faze him at all; he was in his early thirties while I was still in my late twenties.

He actually brightened my day and made me laugh.

He said he had split up from his girlfriend recently too.

We exchanged telephone numbers and kept in touch.

My children thought he was funny, as he would play fight with them like a big kid.

One evening he popped round with some videos and introduced me to a comedian, Lee Evans. I honestly had never laughed so much in all my life.

He reminded me of Norman Wisdom, the actor.

I loved to watch Norman Wisdom films when I was growing up in the foster home.

I could relate to him always being the outcast and messing things up.

Norman Wisdom made me feel NOT ALONE and made me feel it wasn't just me who messed up.

Everyone seemed to have the perfect family and life.

So coming across Lee Evans was like FINDING GOLD and I could not get enough.

I love to laugh and anything that made me laugh, you could count me in.

Our friendship lasted about five months as I encouraged him to get back with his girlfriend, which he did.

I said out of respect it would be best if we didn't hang out anymore.

If he happened to be in the neighborhood he would knock and say hello but that was it.

One day he knocked and I was up to my neck in wallpapering.

I had never done it before personally but I had watched my ex-husband put wallpaper up in our home.

I had promised my daughter that I would wallpaper her bedroom while she was at school.

She had a big cabin bed that I could not move to hang the paper behind.

Perfect timing that he turned up when he did, he helped me pull the bed out so I could hang the last few sheets of paper.

He laughed at me for using my long kitchen worktop as a pasting table. I said, "If you haven't got one, you have to improvise!"

Once I had finished, he helped me push the bed back. It wasn't until he left I then realized that I still had a border to put up.

I managed to do it straight on one side of the room but around the bed it ended up being slightly wonky.

I was disappointed that it was not perfect and in a straight line, but it was the best that I could do.

Once the bed was made, the quilt covered the wonky part of the border anyway.

When my daughter came home from school she looked so happy with her room as she had chosen the wallpaper herself.

Seeing her big smile on her face made me feel so PROUD that I was able to make her happy.

We enjoyed living in our flat and it was handy that all the rooms were on one level because it made it easier for me to keep an eye on everyone.

I started work at my children's infant school helping during the lunchtime break. I helped the children get their food and monitored them after lunch in the playground.

This job fit in perfectly around my children and the school holidays.

My girls made some lovely friends on our road and their school friends all lived nearby.

Our front door was always open to any of my children's friends who wanted to hang out with them.

I looked after my friend's children after school a couple of days a week.

This summer I decided to take my children away for a caravan type holiday.

We had a wonderful time and met up with some friends. The beauty of these holidays was that entertainment was included on site.

After our break away it was time for me to sort out my girl's school uniforms, something that was very expensive the older they got.

I called my girls dad to see if he would help me with the cost of their uniform.

I don't know if I caught him on a bad day, but he was very off and short with me saying, "Don't call me at home. The answer is no. I give you money so get it out of that."

I put the phone down with tears in my eyes, but tried to keep it in so my children wouldn't see me upset.

I made their dinner and bathed them so they were ready for bed.

They each had ten minutes with me on their own before they went to sleep.

They knew not to disturb me while I was spending quality time with each of their sisters.

They could choose how they spent their ten minutes with me. They often chose different things. One may have chosen for me to read a book or they may choose to read it to me. Sometimes they would ask me to make up a story that would include them in the storyline. Or they may choose to sing or just chat about their day.

They each VALUED their ten minutes with me and it made them feel IMPORTANT and special; it was as if the world stopped for them and no one would disturb us.

They enjoyed having my attention and not having to fight for it.

Once a month we would sit down on the floor and share if we had anything on our mind.

I explained to my daughters that if they didn't share how they FEEL then I wouldn't always know, especially if I was busy and preoccupied.

I tried to instill the basics and explained to them that if they did not have MANNERS then, they were NOTHING. I felt this was important for self-worth and with relationships that they would have with others, as life is about sharing ourselves with others.

I didn't want to tell my children off in a manner where they were just told to go to their room. I never wanted my girls to feel REJECTED, no matter what they had done during the day.

Whatever happened in our family, we faced as a family. No secrets. This was not the same as intruding on their privacy.

I wanted my girls to feel SAFE enough to be able to tell me anything. I wanted them to feel SECURE and to be able to TRUST me no matter what.

I would not be cross with them for telling me the TRUTH. I would be more cross about them LYING to me.

I knew parenting was about feeding and clothing and providing a safe environment externally, but what I focused on, was guiding and nurturing them from inside out.

It is easy to tell a child off and say – STOP doing that! Or NO just stop asking!

I would take it further by explaining why I was saying No to them. Yes, it was a long-winded way of bringing them up. It was not a quick fix and took up more of my energy and time.

I knew that by putting them on a naughty step or chair gave them time out ALONE but I didn't want them to feel alone so I HELD them.

It took all my might. I'd have a screaming child on my lap, and I'd be holding them in a cuddling position, with their arms on either side of my body; it was the only way to hold them securely.

This would take anywhere from twenty minutes to half an hour or even an hour.

We would both be sweating after.

I would say to them while I held them, "This is a lovely cuddle." They would scream, "LET ME GO!"

I'd reply back, "When you have calmed down and have stopped crying, then I will stop holding you."

I wanted my children to feel LOVED even when they are upset and angry. I didn't want them to feel alone when they felt like that. The only way that I could share how they felt was get as close to them as I could with a REASSURING CUDDLE.

It was hard work and it was not a quick fix.

But it worked every time.

Once they had calmed down I would open up my arms and say, "You can get off me now."

Each time I'd have the same reaction with every child: they'd choose not to get off my lap. They'd stay and give me a longer cuddle.

When they chose to stop cuddling, they would get off and carry on playing with their toys as if nothing had happened.

Thankfully, because they learnt how to manage their anger, and knew that if they threw a tantrum, I would react with a holding cuddle, there was less point having a tantrum in the first place, and so our communication abilities grew from here.

I know I went about things in a different manner but with so many children to nurture I had to be able to master all their different needs and emotions.

Being a mum is hard work, and attitudes back then were of the mindset *oh are you just a mum, you haven't got a career.*

Well, going to work at times is easier than being a mum twenty-four hours a day.

You get a break when the children nap or sleep but that's that.

At least at work you do clock out but you can't when you have children.

I thought to myself, *The people who said such remarks must not have had the responsibility of looking after children single handedly.*

The government expects mothers to work and they obviously don't recognize how important bringing up a child is. On paper it may seem a good idea but in real life when you don't have a family for support, finding childcare isn't easy.

Working around school holidays created more stress in my family than the work itself.

Over the years, it seemed to me, that families weren't being, supported by the government. They seemed more intent at separating them.

Children are the future and if they are not valued and nurtured, which starts in the home, then rebellion of what they are denied could occur.

It is not about how many adults or children are in the family, it is about support.

Adults as well as children are denied and not encouraged to pursue their unique gifts. Instead we are taught to follow what is set and to fit in; if you don't then you could be an outcast. Schools do not encourage us to fulfill our talents, we are encouraged to follow a set subject matter regardless of if we are good at it or not. Our natural talent does not always have a class in which to join.

Our systems have not helped or encouraged growth it has stunted and repressed talents out of fear, even if that fear started out because being unique is not understood. Some people are good at exams and not so practical, some may not be good at exams and yet know the material. How we express ourselves under the guidelines that are set leaves a lot of talent falling through the systems.

I realized I could not change the system, but I had a choice to not follow it and instead follow my heart. We can be taught something but not really understand it. We are encouraged to memorize it. A lot that is taught relies on memory. This is not the same as natural talent. The thinking brain encourages us to think rather than process what we feel.

I made sure that outside influences and programs would not affect the nurturing I gave my children like rules that were set at school. When my daughter got bullied, she got excluded rather than the bullies, and so I would have to explain to my daughter why it was not personal towards her but reflected on the system,

We did hit many challenges but luckily my children were not alone because they had each other as nurturing back up. They were all close.

As a family we swam against the wave to keep what our family valued and believed in intact.

We did this by always being honest and speaking the truth.

We were honest with ourselves and with everyone else, knowing where they stand and did not have to rely on guesswork.

In some ways being an orphan gave me a clean state to work from.

I was able to create how I would imagine my family should be, one built from a place of love and not material goods or money.

Building a family took more than just getting a roof over our heads or food in our bellies or even finding a job.

I wanted to build my family on something that lasts and doesn't wear out.

Money comes and goes just like friends do.

Places to live are only as homey as you are.

Material goods break down and need replacing.

Appliances once were built to last so they didn't need replacing; now things are made not from a place of value but cheaply for a profit.

This creates a throw away style of living.

Nurturing from a place of love is self-sustaining.

Master yourself then you master your life.

If you are taught to ignore yourself and your feelings then growth is LIMITED.

A life of repeating habits is all that is recycled.

A loving, understanding space is the most valuable gift you can offer anyone so they feel safe to be THEMSELVES.

Fitting all this into a day was exhausting; it didn't leave me any time for myself.

The only way for me to have some me time at the end of the day was to go to bed late.

Once I had finished seeing to the children and the housework, it would be around 10pm before I was able to sit down.

I would do one hour of exercise in my lounge, which helped me to wind down.

I would have a lovely bath then watch some TV or read a book in bed.

One particular night after putting my girls to bed, I didn't bother doing my exercise. I was still upset after my conversation with their dad about the school uniform.

I didn't know how I was going to be able to pay for everything.

I felt so EMOTIONAL and a FAILURE to my children.

I started to run a warm bath and got some wine out of the cupboard that had been sitting there for many months. I wasn't really a wine drinker and didn't really like it, but it was all I had to NUMB the pain that I felt.

I started to cry as I drank my first glass feeling OVERWHELMED and WORN OUT mentally, emotionally, and physically.

Drinking the wine didn't numb my painful feelings, so I got a knife to punish myself.

As a child I had been so used to being physically punished it had became my RELEASE valve.

Growing up, I found that when adults were angry, they took it out on me. I covered this in my first book *From Both Sides of The Fence, The Gifts in U.*

When I was ANGRY with myself, I too took it out on me.

When my girls where angry I CUDDLED them.

I did not want them to be like me and self harm as a release.

I didn't have anyone in the house to punish me so I had to do it to myself.

As I lay in the warm bath while drinking the wine, I decided to use the knife. I cut my wrists, not as a cry for help, as it was a mere scrape, just enough for a RELEASE.

I thought all the children were fast asleep in bed and that the coast was clear.

I was busy in my thoughts and just as I cut my wrists and as the blood trickled down into the bath water, I suddenly heard, "Mum."

My eldest daughter just stared at me.

She asked, "What are you doing?"

I just said I had something stuck in my skin like a splinter and that I was trying to get it out.

I rinsed the blood from my wrist and quickly got out of the bath to tend to my daughter and make sure she was ok.

I tipped the wine down the sink and put a dressing on my wrist before going to bed.

I made sure I never did that again; I didn't do it to try and kill myself or anything, I just wanted a quick release, from now on I would have to find another way to manage my FEELINGS.

The next day I got a call from my girl's dad to say he would go half with me on their uniform but to not tell his wife.

I was RELIEVED he would help.

I left my lunchtime job with the school, as it wasn't much money and the hours being in the middle of the day were not convenient.

I knew I needed to find another job, as I didn't want to be reliant on anyone.

I walked across the road and asked in the bakers if they had any jobs going.

Funny enough they were looking for someone to do a sandwich round and I told them that I had experience.

The hours were great as I didn't start until just after 9am and this gave me a chance to drop my children off to school.

The only problem I had was that my youngest daughter was only at reception half days.

I found a child minder with prices that I was able to afford, and she was able to pick my daughter up at lunchtime and have her a couple of hours until I finished work.

At the end of a working day, my boss would give me spare rolls or bread and cakes and my children loved it.

One day my youngest daughter said to me that she had been locked in the car with the other children while the child minder went inside a shop.

My daughter felt SCARED and didn't like being at the child minders house.

I asked my boss if I could bring my daughter with me to work on my rounds.

KINDLY, she didn't mind and said it was ok. Being a mum herself, I guess she knew what it is like. I was so THANKFUL to have an UNDERSTANDING boss.

I told the child minder that I would no longer need her services; I didn't tell her what I knew, I just said my situation had changed.

My daughter was HAPPY and enjoyed meeting all the people on my rounds, some even gave her a little money.

Once my youngest daughter started school full-time she no longer needed to ride with me.

My boss asked if I would like extra hours to work in the shop after I had finished my round.

I agreed and asked my eldest children to meet me at the shop while I quickly picked up my youngest from school.

I loved working there as it was only at the bottom of my road and my boss was so kind and understanding.

I also had the idea of doing an ironing job, as it was something I could do from home.

Through word of mouth I got three clients a week. I would collect the black bags of clothes and do their ironing until midnight.

How I survived on about 4-5 hours of sleep I don't know with working so many jobs and running a home.

I had starched crisp shirts and piles of clothes all neatly hung and pressed around my home.

I did this for about a year and it put me off doing any ironing for the rest of my life.

While on the sandwich round a young man asked me if I would like to go out for a drink.

I said I would, as he always seemed nice and chatty when I stopped off at his place of work during my round.

My weight went up and down depending on my emotions and stressful situations.

One thing with doing a sandwich round was I didn't have to worry about my weight.

My 30th birthday was fast approaching and I didn't want it to come and go without anything to REMIND me of this milestone.

With no other adults in my life, it was down to me to treat myself. I decided that I wanted to get a tattoo to mark my 30th birthday.

I found a tattooist that was not too far away.

On the Saturday before my birthday I drove us all to the tattoo shop.

The front door to the shop was wide open so we walked straight in. There were chairs in a line around the edges of the small room, with a small table in the middle with tattoo books on it.

I hadn't even decided what design I would like.

I looked at all the pictures that were displayed on the walls.

A dark haired man wearing a leather jacket started to talk to me.

He was coming in for his third tattoo. I explained that it was my first as a GIFT to myself for my 30ᵗʰ birthday.

I asked him if it hurt and he didn't think it did.

With three people in front of me, the wait was going to be LONG, something that I had not planned for.

I took my girls across the road to a sweet shop. My girls were MAD for the popular female band the Spice Girls so I got them each a Spice Girls sticker book and stickers.

I got them something to eat and a drink.

They could not wait to get back to the shop. I felt SORRY for the dark-haired man with my three girls talking so excitedly as they showed him their stickers.

The tattooist popped his head out of his room and called the next person in.

The lady sitting opposite us was nervous as she was having a big butterfly tattoo and she had never had a tattoo before either.

About half an hour later, the tattooist called the lady in.

Not long after, we could hear a commotion from inside the room.

The lady had fainted and so they could not finish her tattoo.

The tattooist sat the lady down and placed a fan on her and she sat and recovered in the waiting room.

He asked for me to follow him into his room and I asked if I could bring my children in with me but he said I couldn't.

I asked the dark haired man if he would mind looking after them while I had my tattoo done.

He KINDLY said, "Of course. No problem."

As I write this, I THINK the world must have FELT more trusting to me back then or I was very naïve and stupid.

I did trust my heart and I did trust my girls. I knew my eldest two daughters would soon call out or come into the room if they needed me.

I was only through a door into the next room anyway.

I didn't know what to expect to be honest. I chose a dolphin as my design and asked him to put it on my shoulder.

It felt like a SHARP JAGGED piece of glass being SCRAPED up and down my skin.

It wasn't that bad but you did feel it.

I wanted the tattoo so much SYMBOLICALLY that I would not have cared how much it hurt.

It didn't take the man long to do it and I felt such a BUZZ after. I was happy with my 30th birthday gift to myself and I had a big SMILE on my face.

I said an ENTHUSIASTIC thank you to the dark haired man for looking out for my girls. I really APPRECIATED it.

He nodded and said, "No problem at all", and walked past me to enter the room.

Some people would say to me, "What have you gone and done that for, scarring your body?"

I didn't see it like that as this had MEANING to me and was the start of my physical self-discovery.

It didn't affect me how my tattoo was JUDGED, it didn't matter how HARSH the reaction; it would not change how PROUD I felt.

I went out on a date with the young man from the sandwich round.

He was a lot younger than me and my friends joked with me saying, "You have landed yourself a toy boy."

He was seven years younger than me and that's nothing compared to the twenty years between my mum and dad. Admittedly my dad was older and not my mum.

It was nice to have some company and I enjoyed the benefits that came with seeing him.

Well, a woman does have INTIMATE needs!

Three months into seeing him, I had the biggest SHOCK of my life; I found out that I was pregnant.

I had no plans to have any more children, as my youngest was now nearly four years old.

I didn't think I would fall as it hadn't happened with my last husband and we hadn't even been careful.

I told him the news and he tried to say that it wasn't his.

I said, "I haven't slept with anyone else, only you."

I had the early scans because of my previous experiences with the molar pregnancy.

I was not prepared for this at all.

Talk about everything happening at once! My daughter's dad was getting married and they were invited to his wedding.

I gave up my sandwich round because of carrying so many heavy bags up and down the stairs.

I felt my sort-of-boyfriend was in denial about being the father of this pregnancy because he was so young and it was the last thing on his mind. We didn't talk about contraception because it was more lust than love.

I decided no matter how he felt, I would keep it as I had three children already and one more would add to the beautiful family that I already had.

I showed my daughters the pictures of my scan and they were excited to be having a new baby brother or sister, even though this wasn't planned.

I felt EXCITED and blessed that I could still fall pregnant being nearly thirty-one.

It all got too much for the baby's father so he didn't have much to do with me.

I felt SCARED having another baby, as I had never experienced a pregnancy on my OWN.

I felt scared but excited at the same time.

My daughter's ages being ten, eight, and four, I hadn't kept any baby things, and so it was like starting all over again.

I had a brain wave and decided to go to a car boot sale that had a good reputation of being good quality.

I went the next Sunday with my friend and I got baby bedding and most things I would need for twenty pounds.

It all looked brand new. I was so HAPPY with my baby bargains.

At sixteen weeks pregnant, I had to have a blood test the results came back that I was a high risk of having a child with Downs Syndrome.

I agreed to be booked in for an amniocentesis and it was explained to me that there is a risk of miscarriage.

This was because they insert a long needle into your womb to draw out some of the amniotic fluid so they can test it.

I agreed and trusted that it all would be fine.

I felt like I was going through life in a DAZE. With so many emotions I felt like I was functioning through life on AUTOPILOT.

Because the father of this child didn't want to know, I asked my best friend to come with me on the day of the test.

I was pumped with ADRENALIN due to being so STRESSED.

I had started smoking because he smoked; it made me feel not so ALONE as it was the only thing I could HOLD on to that he did.

On the day of the test I didn't even feel scared. I just wanted the test over and done with.

The midwife looked at my womb on the screen while the nurse inserted a long needle into my womb.

I was so focused on the screen that I didn't even have a chance to feel the needle.

The midwife asked me if I would like to know the sex of the baby.

I said that I did.

She said a girl.

I was so HAPPY as she would fit in perfectly with my three girls that I already had.

Before we left, the nurse said that I should take it easy and rest as much as I could for the rest of the day.

No lifting or any exertion.

As we pulled up outside of my flat the father of the baby turned up ANGRY and started to chase me down the road. He was angry because he was carrying on an argument from the day before but luckily my children were at school while all of this was going on. I ran while holding my bump with my hands.

I didn't even have a chance to rest with so much drama going on.

Once he left, I went inside and put my feet up and hoped that I would not have a miscarriage.

Luckily as each day passed, I knew that my baby was strong and stayed inside of me.

I had to wait three weeks for the results of the test, which would take me to over twenty- one weeks, which is over half way.

The nurse told me that if I didn't want to keep my baby then I would have to be induced and go through the birth.

I had already decided even if she had been diagnosed with Down's Syndrome I would keep her. We had been through so much together already that I felt so much LOVE toward her.

During my antenatal check ups, the doctor told me it would be best to not try and give up smoking especially as I smoked ten or less, as stress is more harmful to the baby.

Three weeks later I received a letter in the post from the hospital.

I opened the letter and as I read it so quickly that I picked out certain words – DEAR ... WE ARE PLEASED to tell you... NOT DOWN'S SYNDROME.

I was so happy that waiting for the results was over so I could RELAX and start to enjoy my pregnancy.

I let the dad know about his child and that I was carrying a baby girl.

A few days later he called me up to ask if he could see me, as he had time for the news to sink in.

He said he would like to be part of the rest of the pregnancy.

He stayed in touch daily and visited us in our flat while we waited for the birth of our daughter.

December was fast approaching with my due date being the 11th.

I rushed around to make sure I had everything ready for Christmas Day. I knew I would not have time once our baby was born.

On the 30th November I didn't feel right so I decided to put the Christmas tree up once my girls were in bed. I wanted it to be ready for the 1st of December for when my daughters opened their advent calendars. I did this so it would be a surprise for them to wake up to in the morning.

As I put the tree up, my tummy felt funny, it wasn't contractions as such it just felt ODD.

With the last decoration on the tree, I stood back to look at it. I thought it looked a mess.

It would have to do for now. I just didn't feel well enough to change it.

I was awake all night with what felt like waves of contractions.

At 7.30am I decided to tell my baby's father that we needed to go to the hospital. He was staying with us in case I went into labour.

My friend from around the corner took my girls to school. They were so EXCITED and could not wait to meet their new sister.

All I could hear, as I got dressed was MOANING. "This is my day off you have made me get up early. It had better not be a false alarm."

I felt under so much PRESSURE as I knew I would have one ANGRY man to deal with if I did not give birth today.

I had been worried during my pregnancy as I knew each birth got quicker; my last labour had only been half an hour.

I was WORRIED that this one would be even quicker than that.

I had lost so much weight with stress during this pregnancy that I didn't even look pregnant at thirty weeks, but she soon popped out and made up for it DURING the last ten.

At the hospital, a midwife checked me over and said that I was five centimeter's dilated so they would be admitting me.

I was so RELIEVED that it wasn't a false alarm.

The father phoned his mum, who I had met with many times during my pregnancy, to tell her that I was in labour.

A few hours had gone past and a midwife examined me and told me that I had not dilated any more.

I started to PANIC, as I knew he would not be happy with a long labour, as he had already asked how long is it going to take.

From experience I knew that if they burst my waters it would speed things up.

I asked the midwife to break my waters.

In doing so, my contractions came stronger and it wasn't long until I was ready to push.

His mum turned up and came to see us in the labour room but because I was close to delivering our daughter she had to leave the room.

After a few pushes our daughter's head was out, but the midwife had to free the umbilical chord from around her neck.

Finally she was born and she cried for us all to hear.

I could now relax and everyone was happy.

His mum brought my daughters up to the ward so they could meet their new baby sister.

I had a feeling that my new daughter would not have one MUMMY but four.

His mum was at my house looking after my daughters and I relaxed because I knew they were in good hands.

My new baby's father didn't take us straight home from the hospital as he had to pick up his friend and drop him off somewhere first.

His parents had been so SUPPORTIVE. They bought us a lovely pram and his mum stayed with us for a few days to help.

We tried so hard to make it work but the STRAIN of a new baby and with him being young we just didn't see eye to eye.

He would mention my vagina and said that it looked like I had beefsteaks and the landing gear on a plane.

When I told my friend she laughed so much, we did laugh about vagina lips. My motto was to always laugh your way out of situations.

On the surface I could laugh about it, but deep down inside he had planted a seed of INSECURITY.

Not having sisters to compare mine to I didn't know what was termed normal.

I would try to ask my girlfriends about them.

Some would say they had one and my close friend had one and a half, which meant they where different sizes. We use to call them dingle dangles. I am not going to lie they did make me feel SELF CONSCIOUS, especially when my young daughters asked me what was hanging between my legs as I got out of the bath.

Now having a drink was VITAL so I would not feel self conscious about them when having sex.

It was funny because my first love never said a thing neither did my second or third husband so I thought I was normal down there.

I did find them uncomfortable physically with certain garments.

I thought, *Oh well. I can't do anything about them. I was born like this.*

Things got a bit out of hand. I had to get a court injunction and this meant he was unable to come near us for three months.

The first few weeks I found it hard adjusting to having a newborn baby on my own.

After a few months we got in to a routine until she started teething.

One night I was up until the early hours trying to soothe her.

It was about 3 am. I was so tired as I paced up and down in our hallway trying to rock her to sleep.

I suddenly heard my eldest daughter get up from her bed.

I said, "I am sorry if your sister woke you." She held out her hands to take hold of her baby sister.

She told me to sit down and have a drink while she gave me a break. My HEART melted there and then. My daughter was only eleven years old and yet had gotten up to SUPPORT me.

She didn't moan because she had been disturbed and woken up, she just wanted to HELP me.

My daughter gave me her selfless UNCONDITIONAL love.

After I had a cup of coffee I felt refreshed and kissed my daughter as I took her sister from her arms so she could go back to bed.

Thankfully, she was fine after that and we didn't have more late nights due to teething.

As I got back on my feet, I hung out with a friend from around the corner to my flat. After we dropped our children off at school we would meet up for a coffee.

This particular morning I went round to her house. We sat down at her kitchen table and drank our coffee and chatted about our lives.

My friend walked over to her kettle to make us another cup of coffee and a bite to eat.

As the kettle was boiling I said to her that her landline phone was ringing. She looked at me with a puzzled look on her face and said, "No it isn't."

I said, "It is. I can hear it."

Then I realized that it wasn't physically.

But I had heard it as clear as day.

The phone then started to ring loud and clear and so my friend answered it.

It then occurred to me what was happening, my psychic ABILITIES were starting up again.

I just said casually not wanting to make a big thing of it, "Oh psychic phenomena. It happens from time to time.

Her ears pricked up in INTEREST and from here on, the door to my psychic abilities opened UP.

We met up every week. I would tune in to see what came through from the other side.

137

I started to use the word "my love" to address people rather than their birth or known name. My friend noticed how different I became during the reading; she said it was like looking at two different people.

She said I reminded her of Doris Stokes, the medium. I didn't have a clue what she was talking about.

I managed to get hold of Doris Stokes books and I started to read them. I found her story fascinating, as she was a mum too.

Our children would be breaking up for the summer holidays soon, and so my friend and I made the most of the time we had.

We sat outside on her doorstep smoking our cigarettes.

A man from the flats across the road called out to say hello to my friend.

I asked her who he was, she said, "Oh he is such a lovely man. He has three children and is divorced." Her face then lit up and she said, "You two would get on. Let's put your phone number on a piece of paper and put it through his letter box."

I said, "No, you can't go round there and intrude."

My friend would have none of it and marched over to his front door to post my number through.

I tried to not think anymore about it. It felt a bit forward for me, as I don't go around chasing men.

A few days later my phone rang and it was the man who lived across the road from my friend.

Thankfully, our conversation flowed and after chatting for a few days we both felt so COMFORTABLE like we had known each other for years not days, and he invited me round to his house for a drink.

My three daughters were at their dad's for the weekend, so I went round with my seven month old.

He welcomed us both in with open arms.

He had made an effort with the presentation of the cold fruit flavoured drinks and we chatted and ENJOYED getting to know about one another.

He didn't bat an eyelid when I told him about my past. I equally didn't when he told me about his.

It was REFRESHING to meet someone who didn't judge me or hold my past against me.

We spent a lot of time together and my girls loved him, .He worked as an electrician and, being a lot older than I, he was used to being a proper family man, having three children of his own.

He would spend more time at our flat than he would his own and would only stay at his to go to sleep as he lived on his own and his children lived with their mum.

After a few weeks, he asked me to marry him, and I said yes. We just hit it off and got on so well.

Talk about a whirlwind relationship! Our souls just clicked.

Our children between us were bridesmaids. We had such a lovely wedding day. We also managed to get our child minder to stay while we went away for the night.

As a family we had so much fun. His youngest daughter would stay with us every other weekend. His older children worked and would pop in to see him and did not need a weekend arrangement. It helped that they all knew each other from over the school before we met.

We would sing along to our favourite songs in the garden until it got dark.

Life was very noisy and never dull.

I started to do tarot readings and people really LIKED them. I did them over the phone and also face-to-face. I enjoyed doing them because I would tune in beyond reading the meaning of the cards.

From word of mouth, I got busier and booked them in around the children.

I worked evenings, as my husband would be at home.

After the wedding, the three-month court injunction was up and my youngest daughter's dad was allowed to see her.

At first it was advised that he should have supervised visits in a room. I didn't want this for my daughter.

I decided to go with my GUT INSTINCT and give him a chance.

They say absence can make the heart grow fonder and it did in this case.

I did the right thing by listening to my heart rather than my hurt feelings around the past situation.

He had MISSED his daughter so much and had sorted himself out.

We made arrangements between ourselves that he would see his daughter every other weekend.

We shared parenting and he could not do enough for her and I could not fault him. Our friendship and loyalty as parents grew from there on out.

He never let us down or messed us about and continued to always be there if we ever needed him.

He went on to meet a woman with three children and our daughter adapted to his new life.

I managed to have a quiet moment with my husband while the children were asleep in their beds.

I asked him what he thought about booking a holiday abroad.

He thought it would be a great idea and he knew his youngest daughter would love it. His older two children were independent and working.

I booked a one week all inclusive package holiday to Spain for the following year so it would give us enough time to pay for it.

Sometimes our children would muck about when they went to bed by poking their heads from around their bedroom doors.

They thought I couldn't hear them with the television on in the lounge.

I got up and said, "If you girls don't want to go to sleep, that's fine. Get out of bed and to come and stand in the hallway."

They didn't know what to make of it.

I asked them to stand up and that it was fine if they didn't want to sleep but they would have to stand there without making a sound if they wanted to be up.

At first they thought it was FUNNY but after about twenty minutes they started to COMPLAIN that their legs were ACHING.

I said , "If you are tired and don't want to be up anymore, then go to bed."

They realized being up was no longer fun and one by one they went back to bed to sleep – peace at last. My husband left it to me and was quite happy with how I handled the situation.

I tried to be fair and fun but if enough was enough, I meant it.

I would give them THE LOOK – a stare that would be enough to tell them to stop.

Or I would count to ten. I never got to ten because the tone of my voice was enough.

One morning while they sat indoors bored, I came up with a game to play.

I called the girls around me and said, "Who wants to play roles reversed?"

All their EXCITED voices said at once, "Meeeeee! I do."

So I said, "Right now, you're going to be the grown ups for the day. If I need a drink or something to eat, you will make it."

This game lasted half of the morning but at least they got to experience what it was like for us to look after them even if they forgot straight away.

When the game was over I wrote some words on a piece of paper and put them inside one of my socks.

They each took a piece of paper from my sock and whatever was written on their piece of paper, they had to go and find the item.

Whoever came back the quickest with finding their item would pick another piece of paper to find more.

They loved this game and would get a treat after all their hard work. The hard part was getting them to put everything away.

In the meantime my first ex-husband wanted to see his children every other Sunday instead of the whole weekend.

He was still being difficult with paying the forty pounds for his children and it covered nothing. He was back to making me wait and having me constantly to remind him. Although his business was booming he didn't ever put the payment up over many years even though children get more expensive.

On my third daughter's birthday, her dad didn't drop her birthday card off for her. He just said, "When I pick them up next week, I will give it to her then."

He only lived ten minutes from our house and he could have easily dropped in rather than making her wait.

It just didn't make her feel IMPORTANT I guess.

I was HEARTBROKEN for her I played it down to spare her feelings even though to a child their birthday is only once a year and their special day.

I tried to avoid him as much as I could and thankfully my husband would pick up the children from their dad's house if he was too busy to drop them home.

When my daughters came home after being at their dad's, they told me how they had to sit and watch holiday videos of their dad and stepmother swimming with dolphins.

I felt SAD for my girls. He had said he would take them away on holiday with them but it never happened.

Who does that? Who gloats about a holiday that they leave children out from?

I just didn't understand them at all. I could never leave my children out.

This reminded me of the time before I met my husband, when it was bonfire night.

Their dad dropped them home, while his wife's children were saying, "We are going to a fireworks display, you're not."

My heart SANK for them. I didn't have a car and I only had five pounds to my name.

I thought, *There is no way my girls are missing out on watching fireworks.*

I only had one small foldup type of buggy that I used for my youngest.

I knew the three miles there and back would be too far for my daughters to walk.

So I had a bright idea of tying a bed sheet to the back of the frame of the buggy to make it into a hammock.

I sat my youngest into the hammock while my eldest sat on the main seat of the pushchair with her sister on her lap.

This stopped the pram from falling over.

It worked and I managed to get all my children on this tiny pushchair.

We walked to the local display and I paid the five pounds at the entrance.

I was thankful that it was five pound per adult and the children went in free.

I knew I would not have any money for snacks or drinks so I packed a goody bag of sweets and a drink to take with us.

I felt SAD they would not be able to go on any rides or buy anything from the stalls, but I explained to them before we went that we were only going for the firework display and that was that.

We had a wonderful evening. I looked at the big smiles on my daughter's faces and I was PROUD that they hadn't missed out.

I am DETERMINED when it comes to my girls and if I can find a way, I will.

I wasn't looking forward to the three mile, walk back home, especially in the dark of night.

With three tired daughters in the pram, I pushed the pushchair as fast as I was able.

As we got closer to home some children threw a firework that just missed us. I was RELIEVED when we walked through our front door.

The next morning I could hardly walk. I was so TIRED but it was worth it.

Soon after my third wedding, our mutual friend from around the corner invited me out to a gay club with her gay friends.

I had never been to a gay club before and so I didn't know what to expect.

I was expecting it to be just full of gay women and was surprised to see both.

I danced my ass off knowing I would not get hassled by men. I loved the FREEDOM of being able to just dance without SEX or GENDER getting in the way. My friend and I were the only straight women in our group and that didn't seem to offend anyone.

I went to the toilets and noticed that I had been dancing bare foot non –stop. The soles of my feet where black when I got home. My husband he said it sounded like my drink had been spiked. I don't know how as I hadn't noticed anything. Whatever I may have been given, it gave me so much energy.

We continued to see more of our gay friends.

We all went out one day while our children were at school.

It was a warm sunny day and I sat on the backseat of my friend's car and heard a buzzing sound and noticed a wasp was in the back with me.

I PANICKED and SHOUTED for her to STOP the car and that I had to get out They were driving round the roundabout, still panicking, and I opened the car door while saying, "I have got to get out." They started screaming, telling me to shut the car door.

After what seemed like forever, the car finally stopped. I got out of that car so quick. They weren't ANGRY with me, as they could not stop LAUGHING in disbelief of what lengths I would go to get away from a wasp!

We all got on well and one of the gay friends went on to share her stories about being gay.

How women knew what women want.

She told me how she had been with a married woman.

She said anyone can be gay they just don't like to admit it.

I must admit I agree with her, as indifference is only a state of mind.

And to be close and naked with another is more than the mind. It is about being comfortable as well as the pleasurable feelings.

It would explain why many drink to numb the mind and at times feelings.

Really it is about feeling comfortable, especially if you don't feel confident in your own skin. If someone makes you feel safe, it makes it easier to fall in love!

So is sex, really just about sexual organs after all?

It took me back to the time when I shared a double bed with my niece at sixteen years old.

I remembered noticing how different we looked even though we where both female.

I remembered when I shared a bed with a friend and how safe she made me feel.

Who knows what can happen, especially if you get lost in the moment and have had a drink or spend lots of time with someone. You start to see them past their gender.

Maybe if we had not been taught about sexuality and gender then we would see people as people and not what's between their legs.

After all, we are not dogs and don't need to sniff each other to know if we want to have sex.

Soon after, our gay friends relocated to a different area, so we didn't see them anymore.

Society puts thoughts in our heads before we have even had the chance to explore them for ourselves. We are taught to be what we are told we are.

I feel people would be more relaxed about sex if it had not been abused and sold for profit or denied because it is labeled as evil.

How can anyone judge another, especially if you have no experience in what is being labeled and judged?

As a species we are curious and want to know but are often too AFRAID to ask.

If you ask, will it mean you're one too?

I have always been open and honest about sex with my children.

There is a lot I don't know and so there is always more to explore if you wish.

Bottom line: why should we feel bad or wrong for discussing subjects?

The reason is FEAR in case it is catching.

Well, nothing is catching. What you experience is your choice.

There are many outdated recycled labels that are now used to manipulate for power or control.

It would be lovely if adults could treat each other like children do in INNOCENCE.

Why should sex cross the boundaries of your career or AFFECT your career?

Why are our personal lives not personal and RESPECTED? Everyone wants the same things at the end of the day: to live in PEACE. To be understood instead of tied up in labels.

I am THANKFUL for every person that I have met because it is has stopped me from being NARROW MINDED out of lack of experience.

Experience expands the mind with UNDERSTANDING.

I am an open book because I like to WELCOME anyone I meet with open arms.

I soon realized fitting in isn't what it's CRACKED up to be as it comes with a PERSONAL price.

Our gay friends moving away made me want to move. I managed to find a woman who wanted to do a house exchange with me.

Six weeks later, we were set to move on Wednesday 6th December.

Talk about it all happening at once! I had to make sure I had done my Christmas shopping as I knew moving would take up most of our time.

An elderly neighbour had Norma our cockatiel bird for us as she already had one of her own.

My third daughter was sad to leave her bedroom that we had painted like a space ship with lots of glow in the dark stenciled stars.

The house we are moving into had a smashed lounge window and a broken pane of glass in the kitchen.

It had no carpets, only the original concrete flooring.

We moved all our boxes over and placed them into the rooms where they would be unpacked.

We didn't mind about the state of the place, we were just EXCITED at having a house.

My girls decided what rooms they would have.

I had the second biggest room with my husband.

Two of my daughters shared one room while the youngest two had the biggest room.

We decided that we would paint the whole house while the girls were in bed through the night.

It took us ten days to COMPLETE, just in time for Christmas. How we lived on two hours of sleep every night, I don't know. We made a great team, my husband and I. We had a deep connection.

We could not afford carpet or flooring so we used a big rug from our flat to put down in the lounge.

We just told the girls to keep their slippers on.

The first weekend after we moved in was hectic. I went to the toilet and noticed there was no toilet paper left.

I knew that I had put four rolls that I had bought on the side in our bedroom.

I called out to one of my girls to pass me the toilet rolls.

My daughter replied saying that there were no toilet rolls in my room.

My husband was at work half day, so I was unable to ask him.

I asked if one of my daughters would walk to the shops at the top of our road to buy some toilet rolls.

I was stuck on the toilet so I asked them to get some coins from out of my purse, and I waited, sitting on the throne until they returned.

I was THANKFUL for them going.

I heard the front door open and my daughter ran up the stairs to give me them so I could get off the toilet.

I placed a toilet roll into the holder and after flushing and washing my hands, I looked in my bedroom to where I had left the toilet rolls the day before.

When my husband came home I explained to him what had happened and he was as confused as I was since he had seen the four-pack of rolls on our side in our bedroom as well.

We looked everywhere in our house but they were nowhere to be found.

The next day I got up to get dressed and on the side were the toilet rolls that had gone missing the day before.

I asked my girls if they had been playing tricks with us, and hiding the toilet rolls but they said they hadn't.

I now had plenty of toilet paper! Eight rolls in total.

Psychic phenomena happening again but I wasn't AMUSED because it cost money.

I said out loud, "If you want to get my attention, find another way."

It wasn't uncommon to get many visitors in our house but not physical ones.

An old gentleman with glasses sat on our sofa.

I saw a young child sitting on a hale bale in mid air.

One time I saw a blonde haired girl looking out of the bedroom window. At first I thought it was one of my daughters because of the blonde hair quickly realized it wasn't her..

Murder victims would visit me to tell me their stories.

My daughters had gotten used to the strange happenings in our house.

Sometimes they didn't like it and the phenomena would scare them. If I weren't in the house with them, they would leave the house to stay round their friends for the night instead.

I just told them that our soul friends were looking out for us and letting us know that we were safe.

I would continue to explain that they wouldn't hurt them as they have only ever looked out for us.

Their imagination would run away with them as they didn't always understand it and had listened to too many ghost stories.

I tried to explain to them that they were not ghosts and that they were just like us.

One night I was out and I got a phone call from my screaming girls saying the plates from the kitchen cupboard had fallen from the cupboard in neat piles onto the kitchen floor.

They went on to explain that they were in a different room and had heard the noise come from the kitchen.

Yes, this was a bit extreme but the shelf did need securing, so I was thankful that our soul friends had reminded us, and no crockery got smashed.

It never happened again, we mended the shelf; I am sure it saved an accident from occurring.

I wanted to get more psychic experience and did what is known as *platform* at a spiritualist church and I also worked at a spiritual shop.

It was interesting to observe how other mediums and spiritual people worked.

Some spiritual people I had met were not that spiritual.

Some of the rules and regulations just did not sit with me. I did not agree with the medium being more important than the person the medium was tuning in for.

I soon left these organizations and decided to work on my own and keep myself to myself.

The next summer we had our first family summer holiday abroad.

All our girls were EXCITED. We arrived at the airport and once we were checked in, we got something to eat and looked around the shops.

We all boarded the plane so excited for our holiday adventure.

What a week we had of sun and swimming in the pool, with lots of dancing and singing and entertainment.

Our girls made some lovely friends when they joined in with the poolside activities.

They loved that they could get an ice cream whenever they wanted without needing any money to pay for it being all-inclusive.

The holiday was coming to an end and our girls were SAD to be leaving to go home.

They exchanged telephone numbers with the friends that they had made.

It had been so much FUN that we decided to book another holiday straight away as soon as we got home for the following year.

It meant being extra careful with money but if you want something enough you have to make sacrifices for it to happen.

I ordered a shopping catalogue that came through in the post.

I would look through the catalogue once our children were in bed.

I had a brain wave to get a video camera so we could capture some home movies.

I ordered it because this catalogue made it possible to pay for it weekly.

When it arrived, I showed it to our girls and they thought it was AMAZING and spent many a winter day recording them selves, singing and dancing.

I had to buy lots of blank cassettes; this video camera became our family entertainment.

Unfortunately, the younger members of the family would forget to put a new blank tape in the machine and record over what had been already recorded with zero editing.

When we would watch our home movies the scenes would cut out into another scene.

With winter now over and spring in the air, I decided to surprise our children with a special dinner.

While they were at school, I bought everything that was chocolate or chocolate covered.

I made them a chocolate dinner; I thought it would be a childhood dream.

I came up with the idea because it was Easter.

I had button Easter eggs in the fridge so they would be nice and cold.

I was so excited and could not wait for them to see this chocolate dinner surprise.

As they walked through the kitchen door for dinner their faces did look SURPRISED at all the different types of chocolate treats.

I got the Easter eggs out of the fridge and gave them each a half shell.

I put a scoop of ice cream in each shell.

I said, "You have to try and eat it with a knife and fork or with your hands behind your backs using just your mouths."

After about twenty minutes, my third daughter started to cry and said, "I just want something NORMAL like a jacket potato."

We all LAUGHED and put the chocolate dinner away, it just goes to show that too much of a good thing is just too much.

We never did a chocolate dinner again and stuck to normal food.

I thought it would be a child's dream but giving a child too much just SPOILS the fun.

I LOVED my husband very much and he was like a best friend to me.

I could chat to him about anything and he supported my psychic work. He often came to readings with me.

I also had many clients that would come to my house.

I was unable to do tarot readings anymore because of another phenomena that happened.

After the last tarot reading that I did, I placed my tarot cards and book on the passenger seat of my car. After I pulled up and parked the car outside our house, I turned the engine off and reached across to the passenger seat to pick up my cards and book.

The book was there but the cards were missing.

I knew I had put them on the seat because I had looked at them before I started the car to drive home.

They were not in the car. I looked everywhere and could not find the cards or the drawstring velvet bag they were in.

I was not happy about it but decided that I had no choice but to accept it.

I now had to do peoples readings without any PROPS.

I didn't know how they would work out.

As it happened, it FELT more NATURAL to me and I enjoyed talking to my client's relatives that would CONNECT with me.

Our next family holiday abroad didn't work out quite as well as the last one.

The rain fell so heavily that it flooded our apartments.

Our clothes and shoes got ruined.

We got moved to a different hotel, which ended up being an upgrade, and we eventually had the best time ever.

It was like PARADISE.

People soon heard what I did and some staff came up to me to read their palm. This is what they called it because of the language barrier. So showing the palm of their hand to me they knew I would understand them. I could not and did not read their palms.

On some occasions I had felt a bit TIPSY after having some alcohol. I didn't know how I would do a reading FEELING like this, but I didn't like to say NO to people.

I always wanted to help.

I noticed how being tipsy didn't affect the reading. I would feel tipsy but as soon as I started the reading, I became SOBER and as soon as the reading was finished I became tipsy again.

This was when I realized that nothing in the PHYSICAL would get in the way of a reading or a message.

I hated labels and names. I would say to people, "You can call me whatever you want but to me I am a MESSENGER because that is what I am doing, passing on your message."

Even as we left to get the bus to the airport, a man ran over to me holding out his palm.

I gave him what I could under the circumstances.

When we got home I decided to put in a claim for the many problems that had occurred at our first hotel.

I started to talk to a man that did holiday claims and he gave me some advice, as he went on to advise me that I would not get full compensation because they knock OFF the price of the flights straight away.

I decided that I would put in a claim and do it myself.

I did a statement type letter including photos.

To cut a long story short I did get full compensation and when I told the insurance man he was SHOCKED. He said, "I have been in this business over twenty years and never seen anyone get full compensation." He offered me a job there and then.

I told him that I just knew what I wanted and went with my heart and inner truth as guidance.

I DECLINED his kind offer, as it was not something that I saw myself doing as a job.

I was so happy as it meant I could get a new fitted kitchen, as our kitchen worktops were so small that I wasn't able to put big dishes on them.

We chose our kitchen and my husband fitted it which made it affordable out of the compensation money.

A year later CRACKS started to appear on the surface in my marriage and yet deep down we continued to remain close. These cracks were more to do with not being able to settle inside, and so arguments would occur because of this feeling that is felt inside.

We did everything together and we were very rarely apart.

We often had missions from painting each room more than once, to putting up flat packed furniture, to buying a second hand sofa out of the local paper called the gazette.

Our home was hectic with always something going on.

As our girls grew they also grew out of using the video camera, and so it got put away and replaced with their own mobile phones.

We got our first computer, which they enjoyed using to help them with their schoolwork.

ARGUMENTS would occur over who had taken their makeup or clothes while at the same time DENYING any knowledge of it.

Dee Weldon Bird

My family was FRAYING under the hormones that surfaced like a volcano.

I had a chat with my husband and we decided to split up.

He found a flat not too far away and moved out.

I LOVED my husband so much but something just didn't FEEL right.

I could not even explain it; I just couldn't SETTLE.

We got divorced and although we lived in separate homes, we still continued to see each other every day. And so life in a way was no different from how we began. Nothing much changed apart from living in separate homes. Everything else still stayed the same.

I couldn't believe I was on my third divorce at only thirty-five years old.

It was such a strange situation to be in, to be SOUL connected with someone but yet feel SEPERATED physically.

His youngest daughter moved in with him and it was lovely seeing them spend QUALITY time together.

I would often go around his flat too and we would all chat together.

My ex-husband started seeing someone but wasn't FEELING it, so this was nothing serious.

I began seeing an actor whom I felt a connection with because our childhoods MATCHED. We both had come from the care system and had been in children's homes. Yet as adults our lives could not be further apart, so we met in the middle of FANTASY.

I felt like I had to be super skinny being with him and so I lost a lot of weight.

My weight was something I felt I could CONTROL when my life felt out of control.

I joked with my ex-husband that if we both where still single in ten years time we would get back together.

156

A few days later he found out that his sister was unwell so he visited her at the hospital daily over the next six months and this meant we didn't see each other as often.

We kept in touch by phone just to check in and SUPPORT each other in our lives. We shared what was happening in our personal lives and didn't get jealous because our relationship was more about CARING about one another than sex.

We also had what I call GOODBYE sex more than once. Goodbye sex is not the same as relationship sex.

Even though on paper we had divorced and lived in separate houses, in our hearts we were just as close. You just cannot separate love.

He supported me through every Christmas, when I would feel the SADNESS of losing my mum, as the MEMORY would come flooding back.

He understood why I had to buy lots of presents to keep myself busy.

I would say to him every year, "I hate the 22nd December!" I was always glad when it had passed and Christmas day was actually here.

In the evenings in my spare time I started to write a book called *The World Beyond*.

My ex-husband loved the sci-fi theme and made me PROMISE that I would finish writing a book one day.

I half laughed and said, "I will write it but I doubt it will get PUBLISHED because my grammar is SHOCKING."

He said, "Don't let that put you off. That is what editing is for."

He planted a SEED of thought that day.

The next time I went to see my actor boyfriend I noticed that he had a book laying on the floor. The title read *How to Tell if You Have Been ABUSED*.

It was only a small book and so I started to flip through the pages out of curiosity.

I started to read all the different numbered points.

As I read the first one I thought *YES that's me*, then the second then the third until I got through all of the numbered points. I dropped the book to the floor and a lot of ANGER surfaced from INSIDE of me.

I could not believe I matched up with them all. I had blocked all the details out and separated myself from it. I tried to cover it up when I entered the children's home. Reading this was like connecting myself back to what had happened and owning it.

It was like the floodgates had opened from my past as soon as I had finished reading it.

I was angry at my truth surfacing from inside of my self. This book had triggered my past and I could not close the door on it.

I had separated from my past and therefore had convinced myself that it had happened to someone ELSE and not me.

I had BLOCKED it out and had only been left with certain triggers on certain months like the month of December.

I was determined to make sure Christmas was fun and full of magic and happiness.

The complete opposite of my childhood memory, and made sure I DISTRACTED myself by putting lots of ENERGY into it.

I focused on FUN, which blocked out my feelings of SADNESS and it WORKED.

Then my ex-husband had some sad news that his sister had passed away. He felt sad but was happy that he had the chance to spend time with her and made their PEACE with each other.

We still continued to go to the cinema every Wednesday. I loved going to the movies and escaping everyday life. .

My relationship with my actor boyfriend was COMPLICATED to say the least.

I loved the FANTASY element but equally missed the traditional type of sex. as it was all about fantasy rather than the act of sex.

Why is it if you choose something that is DIFFERENT, it means you give up something that's in its place.

I had noticed this with many different situations. I often thought to myself, *Why do you have to choose? Why can't you have BOTH?*

I didn't see my boyfriend that often, maybe once a month. Half of me felt like I was a part-time girlfriend with BENEFITS.

It was nothing like the long-term relationships that I had been used to all my life.

This was like something out of a movie script.

I didn't get invited to functions and see him as often, as a relative had moved in with him.

I felt sad and PUSHED OUT and REJECTED like an out of date toy.

It was a very VOLATILE relationship, full of highs and lows. He was stuck in his past while I was trying to move away from mine. We clashed while meeting in the middle of fantasy. I wanted him to feel loved while he had a battle with it. Trying to love someone who is in battle and in protection mode is not easy.

I noticed how his relative's skin was whiter than mine and my boyfriend had dark skin yet they both had one dark skinned parent.

This made me think that the argument on racism is silly as you could look at a white man and yet they are half black, but your eyes cannot see it.

This is why it is important to get to know people before passing judgment.

Eyes can DECIEVE you.

I feel we are all skin tones, just some SURFACE through generations and some don't.

My part-time boyfriend even mentioned the shape of my vagina. He spoke as if he had never seen a vagina like mine before, a judgment that COMPOUNDED my INSECURITY about my body. I asked my ex-husband what he thought about the lips on MY vagina. He just said they are normal as all women are different, any man that moans about them are obviously not very MATURE or EXPERIENCED and INSECURE in THEMSELVES.

He made a great point and one I LIKED.

I still didn't feel comfortable in my own skin.

A friend had told me how she had an operation to trim hers. I was INTRIGUED and fascinated that such an operation was possible.

Sex comes naturally to wild animals and all animals come to think of it.

They don't have hang ups or worry even who is watching.

Sex is purely an act in which to keep a species going.

Are humans the only ones that participate in sex for PLEASURE?

I had a lady come to my house wanting a psychic reading.

Her first boyfriend came through. He had passed years ago in a motorbike accident.

He came through wanting to let her know that he was ok.

Well this next experience was like the film Ghost and I allowed him to use my body to EMBRACE her during the reading, with me being piggy in the MIDDLE.

I CONNECTED like a bridge between them.

When they hugged each other, I felt what they felt as they TRANSFERRED their energy to one another.

Wow! It was like I had never had sex in my life. It was more than an ORGASMIC feeling. This experience answered a question that I had. Do souls have sex in the afterlife?

The answer is yes, through energy transfer as they connect, rather than a physical act.

This energy travelled through every cell of my body.

The lady who came for the reading felt it too.

We both where BLOWN AWAY

It was something I haven't experienced again since.

After this experience, it fired my INTEREST in energy and connection past the flesh and bones.

I remembered how I used to play with my own energy when I was fourteen. I would FOCUS my energy on my breasts to make them grow a cup size.

At the time, I didn't give it much thought. It was natural to me.

I guess once my breasts were the size I liked I forgot about what I had done.

What comes naturally, you tend to not have to think about.

I already knew that we were not just our physical body.

When I first got married to my third husband, he woke me up one night.

I looked at him standing in our bedroom doorway and he started asking me about what item of clothing would I like to wear, while holding up my bra.

I shrugged, I didn't know, as it was too early; I was still half asleep.

I then heard him snoring next to me in bed.

I quickly turned my head round to see if he was in fact still in bed next to me.

He was naked from the waist up snoring away, oblivious that I was talking to him while he stood in our bedroom doorway.

This CONFUSED me and SHOCKED me. I had been used to seeing dead people – people that had passed and EXITED as I called it.

I knew my husband wasn't dead as he was BREATHING and snoring.

Yet here he stood in front of me fully clothed as real as you and me having a conversation with me.

This experience showed me how we are not our flesh and bones, and how the soul is busy while the physical sleeps.

I UNDERSTOOD how you do not have to wait until your death or exit as I say before you get your soul.

I understood how we already have our SOUL and the soul is over shadowed by the physical, like wearing a VEIL.

You could say that we are in two REALITIES, one being the physical and one being the soul. The challenge is MASTERING the DIFFERENCES between them.

After these experiences I would practice on my husband to see what my own soul was CAPABLE of.

I asked him one day to sit in our kitchen on a dining room chair and I sat opposite him.

I STARED at the top of his head and suddenly I saw his brain inside his skull.

I was so shocked! After that, I started to notice during my readings that I could look inside my client's body. It was like having X-RAY vision and I could see if they had any broken bones in the PAST.

I obviously did not go around looking inside people's bodies. I would only look if asked, if they wanted more INFORMATION on a certain part of their body.

I always said, "I am not a doctor so only take what I say as GUIDANCE and always follow your own doctor's advice."

My husband SETTLED in to living with his daughter in his flat.

Our first Christmas living apart, was actually spent together as my children were at their dad's.

He made me a lovely fresh strawberry breakfast with pancakes.

I felt very LUCKY to have my very special SOUL friend.

He understood me and I felt SAFE with him.

Our situation was a head fuck as we were close and continued to spend most days together yet we where apart.

We didn't split up because we had fallen OUT of love, we were very much still IN love with each other, we had just fallen out of the physical side of our connection.

The next chapter of our lives felt like we were facing the unknown. Or were we?

OVERVIEW

This chapter of my life showed me how love is not black or white.

I experienced how colourful love actually is.

I witnessed how love is MANIPULATED for gain and controlled out of FEAR.

Having children and having so many marriages at such a young age brought ME a DIFFERENT way of LOOKING at love.

I would say love is not only full of SURPRISES and SYNCHRONICITIES it is also UNPREDICTABLE.

I felt like I had DROVE into the DEEP end of love, which covered the SHALLOW end at the same time.

My love life started out as a HELL of a journey as a small child and turned into quite a roller coaster ride that would not end.

I adored my children. They are PRICELESS to me. Even when I child minded I always found it hard to put a price on anyone's HEAD.

I looked for the HEART and DEPTH INSIDE of all people.

My children brought such RICHNESS to my life and yet at the same time I was so POOR.

I was experiencing both sides of the coin you could say, it was the riches in my life that money cannot buy and that was what FUELLED me to keep going and not give up.

I didn't want to TURN my back on love or CLOSE myself off from love.

I told myself when I was a child going through adversity that nothing would be that bad for me to give up on love.

Its been TOUGH don't get me wrong. I even HATED it here and didn't want to be here.

At times I wanted to give up and tried but DEEP down something inside of me would STOP me from going too FAR.

My own DOORMAN in my life is my SELF as well as IT causing my BARRIERS and BLOCKS.

I was thankful that throughout my life many people had pointed out what was CLASSED as wrong with me.

I was told to toe the line and FIT in.

I tried to fit in and I NEVER did.

Having children was my life SAVER here.

My children saved me from my physical self.

I wasn't alone anymore. We became a FAMILY and a TEAM.

I may be older in years but we SUPPORTED each other.

TOGETHER we had all we NEEDED, we just didn't have much money.

This at times caused a DILEMMA for my children, as they would see what they didn't have that other children did.

They saw other children with nice clothes and trendy BRANDED labels. Ours had an important label in theirs, it just happened to be their own PERSONAL NAME.

Money can bring you EXPERIENCES past your wildest DREAMS but it cannot buy you HAPPINESS and if it does, often it is SHORT lived.

SUSTAINING happiness is sustaining your self.

I didn't want my children to get bullied or go through what I did growing up, but you're not going to stop what has been a BATTLE for CENTURIES.

When it comes down to it, it does not matter what you have or don't have, if someone wants to bully they will FIND something.

I taught my children to be STRONG and to have a VOICE, to speak their TRUTH. I always tried to LISTEN to them as well as have them listen to me. Adults don't always listen as I found out as child.

I knew I had a SENSE of self, which physically didn't paint a PRETTY picture.

I now had to SHARE myself not only with MEN that crossed my path but FRIENDS too.

I found friendships didn't always run SMOOTHLY.

Society taught me that if you don't have friends then there must be something WRONG with you.

No one wants to be LEFT OUT or rejected.

In truth everyone while growing up, WORRIES about not having friends. FACING school or any activity on your OWN can feel SCARY.

I was thankful that I did have so many children as I knew they would not be like me in life, alone, as they would always have each other.

Sharing is TOUGH to MANAGE.

I loved my first child so much that I wondered how it would be possible to love MORE than one child.

You do because they are all different and UNIQUE.

This meant I could not type CAST love, I had to EXPAND how I loved my children with their own unique needs.

I noticed even if I could manage their unique needs the children themselves were still trying to manage themselves. Having so many sisters they did naturally fall out and not see eye to eye.

The main frame of love in our family was to UNDERSTAND the MEANING behind the action or word.

Once you understand this then arguments were not taken PERSONALLY.

Disagreements usually BLEW OVER as quickly as they had started.

I was PROUD that we didn't hold grudges for days.

As a child I was EXPOSED while others HID.

I didn't want my children to be AFRAID of who they were.

I didn't want them to feel BADLY for being themselves.

Love for your SELF is challenging enough. To SHARE love is a mission.

I OBSERVED how love could be kept CLOSE to the chest. Love can be ABUSED, and manipulated, discarded, it can be ignored, and rejected. How love is HANDLED looked like to me that it had more value than a POSSESSION, which made people feel valued too.

Love had become a CURRENCY like money, something to barter with and exchange for something in return.

Often an exchange can be at a personal COST.

I wanted to prepare my children so they didn't just follow life like a script and say and do and nod in response to questions or to people PLEASE.

The person that should always come FIRST is YOUR SELF. If you're not happy then you will not be HAPPY in life.

It is your own self -RESPONSIBILTY, to KNOW what you WANT when you share your love with other people in the world.

If you RESPECT and LOVE your own love in YOU, then you WON'T connect with people that abuse it.

You want to connect with people who will treat you how you TREAT yourself.

Sadly life is one big DISTRACTION from your self. My childhood TRAUMA was SWEPT under the carpet in the hope that it made it disappear. Out of sight, out of mind.

Love doesn't work like that. Love is TRANSPARENT and hides from nothing.

Love is in every thought and every action; you cannot delete love or erase it, because love is energy and not a solid material object.

Love is as FREE as the air that you BREATHE even when it is contained inside a VESSEL.

I was TAUGHT that I had to EARN LOVE, to earn TRUST, to earn and work for everything.

Nothing in life is free.

Who made this RULE up?

Love is FREE. The only thing you pay for is the vessel that you SHARE to experience love.

You pay for the meal, the clothes, and the gifts in exchange for love.

The simple things in life are FREE, so why is love made so COMPLICATED and so expensive? It is so you pay for it to PROVE how much it MEANS to you, because it is not BELIEVED or EXPRESSED from the HEART only from the wallet or purse.

I didn't want my girls growing up to feel SCARED of themselves, which starts with the physical BODY.

I didn't hide my physical body from my girls and would not be shy to get out of the bath NAKED and run to my bedroom to get dressed.

My flesh I EXPOSED to them, while we still all RESPECTED our personal SPACE and privacy.

I would not make a big deal of our physical bodies.

LOVE exposes our depth and meaning.

Love will always know your truth behind your actions and words.

I wanted my children to grow up not being scared to have a voice as speaking your truth is respecting the love you have for yourself.

If you feel the need to lie then you deny yourself self-security.

I didn't want my girls to go through life proving themselves like I had to.

I knew the only way to guide my girls to adulthood was to expose the truth about love as it's not always romantic.

To understand love is to understand life in all its glory.

I encouraged them to face life full on and know that they were not always going to be treated how they expect, and that they will be heartbroken and upset.

If you always want to hide your love and run from love then you are not exposing yourself to what love is.

The love you experience is MIRRORED on what you believe about yourself and the world around you.

I exposed how FULL up on love they were and I explained how their cup was not half full or half empty.

I just wanted them to show up to life, turn up and be the best that they could be.

I did not have a grade or standard for them, I felt they would set this for themselves.

I could not put any label on my children's heads. Their names were enough.

I saw their own MAGIC in them, their own personal gifts and skills, something you cannot teach.

I valued the gifts that they exposed and revealed to me.

I noticed how different in character they were and how their, personalities are unique.

This showed me that we are more than blood. If we were just connected in blood then there would be no UNIQUENESS in the world, and we all would be clones.

We are DIFFERENT because we are more than genetics. We are our SOULS.

I equally knew that I could not hide from my past by being distracted with being a parent.

Being a parent had given me some space from my past but it equally revealed to me what I needed to face.

If I were to grow with my children then I had to face myself as much as I encouraged them to face themselves.

This leads me to the next chapter of my life, going back to come forward. If I wanted to create love in life I had to face my past first before I could face my future.

Exposure is not CLOSURE.

CHAPTER SIX

36-39 YEARS

The first few years with my children, I kept them under my wing you could say.

I protected them and guided them and prepared them for the day they would flee my nest.

I held their hands through their experiences, explaining to them the meaning of their actions and words. Understanding yourself does not come under a label of right or wrong or good or bad. Through experience they would know what they like and what they didn't like, and it was OK to know.

The more they understood themselves, the more they would face life and be confident with the decisions and choices they would go on to make.

Life starts with the self not the distractions around you.

At times we all got distracted from situations that were going on around us.

Meeting people is like being in the middle of fireworks at times.

You can control yourself to the best of your ability but you cannot control what other people say or do.

It is easy to take it personally and forget who you are.

Each time my children got pulled into situations that they didn't like I would gently bring them back to themselves and reassure them that they are OK. For example, they may have fallen out with friends, or with trends and social media. As they got older they may have been asked to take drugs and their friends may have thought they were odd if they didn't. I would remind them that no matter what life threw at them, they could face it if they stuck to their own truth.

The arguments that occurred from the school playground started to enter our home through social media apps.

The computer on one hand was a great tool to explore the world around them, from the comfort of their living room, but on the other hand, chat rooms brought the playground arguments home.

We used to be able to shut the door on the outside world, now the outside world was slowly creeping into our family home.

I had a mobile phone and as each child reached senior school they got a phone also. It was a way for me to keep connected with them when they where out and about, it gave me peace of mind that they could get ahold of me if they needed.

Since we moved, the girls had further to walk to school, which included busy main roads.

There had been a few stories on the news of young girls going missing and being murdered.

Stories that make any parent more cautious.

I was happy that my two older girls would walk to school together. They would meet up with other school children that were walking to school as well.

I had my reasons for giving them a phone out of personal safety but my girls wanted a phone because all their friends had one.

Pay as you go worked out more expensive back then. Ten pound a week worked out forty pound a child a month, which never seemed enough.

Everything comes at a cost. If you love something you have to take care of it.

Although we didn't have much money, I would tell them money does not define you, what you love defines you.

I wasn't work shy.

I worked posting catalogues through people's front doors. I had many roads and walked in all weather.

In return I earned minimal money something like twenty pound a week for many hours of work.

I wasn't embarrassed what work I did, a job was a job to me and I would get on with it.

It wasn't about the job for me. It was about providing enough for my children.

I didn't want it all being on my husband's back, and always found a way to work around my children while still bringing them up.

I didn't trust strangers to look after my girls. This stemmed from being in the care system and how I had been abused.

I had my children and they were my responsibility.

Arguments escalated in our home with teenage hormones overflowing, they told me how life was so unfair.

Juggling teenage children is not always easy because, they had grown too big to be under my wing they were now finding their own feet.

I didn't want to control them. I wanted to continue guiding them.

I was out of my comfort zone as it was never just one child letting off steam.

With only one of me, facing my children at times felt like a battle as they each had strong personalities; this showed that I had nurtured them well.

I had to put my foot down and be firm but fair and stick to what I meant no matter how much it hurt me to do so.

I had a small child of four who was at infant school and the others were in juniors and seniors and they all had different needs.

I had toys that took up all our living space downstairs because they were too big to fit in the bedroom.

It had been a long day so I decided to have an early night. I lit a candle and put it on my windowsill next to my bed.

The next thing, I knew my daughter came into my bedroom in the morning and said it smelt of smoke.

I looked at the windowsill and noticed I had not blown out the candle before going to sleep.

I asked my daughter to bring me a cup of water so I could put out the candle, as it would not go out by blowing it.

She handed me the cup of water that she had got from the bathroom. I tipped it over the candle to extinguish it.

The candle exploded like a firework and the flames hit the blinds like I had fired a flaming rocket.

The blinds went up in flames. I suddenly remembered a television advert I had seen as a child and it demonstrated how a house went up in flames in a matter of minutes.

I panicked, thinking we only had two minutes to get out of the house.

I told my girls to get out of the house and to go outside with me so we could get in our car. We called the fire brigade and waited for them to arrive.

I called my ex-husband and he said he was on his way.

All we could do is sit and watch as we saw the flames rise up at the bedroom window.

It didn't look good.

I knew that I had paper posters on the walls on either side of the window, and a floor lamp next to my bed with some clothes hanging from the rim of the shade so they could dry.

I had silk sheets on my bed and watched as the burning blind fell onto my bed. I thought, *Oh no my bed is going to ignite and go up in flames too.*

The firemen arrived quickly and went into my house and extinguished the flames.

Once they knew it was safe to enter the house, they brought us inside and the firemen showed me the damage.

The double-glazed window was smashed in tiny pieces from the heat inside its frame.

The walls were black from the smoke but my posters and clothes were all still intact and there was a small round burn on my bed covers, which looked like a big cigarette burn.

I was so relived.

We opened all the windows to let some fresh air in.

The fireman told me off for tipping water on to a burning candle.

I was already shaken up and I needed comfort, not a telling off. How was I meant to know if I had not been told? They did not teach this kind of thing in school.

It did make me wonder if other people knew how to properly extinguish candles.

I never forgot this that was for sure. Him being cross, made sure I never left a burning candle alight again. And the fact of my home could've gone up in flames made it a great deterrent.

I threw out all my candles and made sure the only type of candle that I would burn from then on were tea lights because burn out after a few hours.

It's one thing seeing fire scenes on the television but seeing it happen right before your eyes is scary.

My ex-husband turned up as the firemen were leaving I said how thankful I was and sorry for not knowing that candles can explode.

My ex-husband took my children to school for me while I started to clean the black from the walls.

When he returned I said, "All it needs is a fresh lick of paint."

Once we had cleaned the walls, we went and got some paint, and I chose a warm pink.

We had just started to paint when my part-time boyfriend phoned me. I told him about the fire and that we were in the middle of cleaning the mess up.

About an hour later he turned up to help us with the painting.

Between the three of us, we got it done in no time.

The only evidence that a fire had occurred in my room was if you looked at the window.

I called the council and they came round a few days later to replace it with a new window.

I was thankful that no one got hurt that day and what did get damaged got fixed and replaced.

I had a big wake up call that day, one that I would live with forever.

I went to bed that night thankful that I had people who helped me in my time of need.

I am sure my children had learnt from my mistake, not to throw water on a burning candle.

After the fire I decided to have a move around of the bedrooms to see if this would help defuse arguments.

I was always changing rooms around as it felt like it gave our life a spring clean with a new outlook, rather than the same old thing, just a different day.

I did not like to be in a rut and if I was, I would not want to stay in it for long.

I decided I would have the smallest bedroom and the two oldest girls had the middle -sized room while my two youngest had the biggest room so they would have room for all their toys.

I gave the girls my double bed and I had a single bed in my room and the older two had bunk beds.

I knew it may have seemed odd, a mum having a single bed but I didn't care as my children always came first.

You only use one side of a double bed if two people are sharing it any way so what was the difference?

I adapted to no longer being married but in my heart, I was divided between the past and the present.

I had my first taste of what it felt like being separated totally from my ex-husband and not included in his life, even if it was for one day.

That one-day was the following Christmas. I didn't see him as he was spending the day with his children. It was our first Christmas apart since we had known each other.

We did meet up on Boxing Day though.

I respected that I was no longer a priority in his life and that our relationship wasn't falling apart at the seams, it was expanding to include others.

It made me realize how much he meant to me, I felt confused how I could love someone so much and yet not be able to settle down. This made more sense later on once I pieced my life together. Looking back, I see how my heart has been ahead of my life, and that the physical was on catch up. It just didn't make sense as it was like we had never split up and yet we were divorced.

We both would sit and talk about our relationship and somehow we understood it and those closest to us understood the love we shared.

It wasn't a normal situation and those that didn't know us very well I am sure would find it very odd.

I started to go to a spiritual circle, which was a meeting with other people who are psychic, so I could meet like-minded people. I met a lady who did healings and she invited us all to attend a healing session that was being organized at her spiritual church.

As a group we decided to attend.

I agreed to turn up although I felt very uncomfortable about anyone getting close to me, as they would find out about my past.

I started to feel agitated as I had spent years hiding my past from my children and kept it locked away so it didn't interfere in my life.

I didn't want to open a door that had been locked for so many years.

I used my psychic abilities part-time around my family and it was a side of me that ran parallel to my physical path in life.

My physical life was my main stage, my main focus and priority because of my children.

My circle of friends were mixed, half of them where because of being psychic, and the other half, because of my personal life.

Both sides didn't always mix very well.

Some people understood me, some got freaked out by me and some just thought I was rude if my heart called me to help someone in need.

This happened once during a night out with my part-time boyfriend.

I had been used to sharing my psychic world with my ex-husband and he accepted this side of me and even encouraged it.

I forgot at times that all people were not as accepting.

I was to meet my half boyfriends close friends and we were meeting at a restaurant.

I know this may sound silly, but I had not really gone out to restaurants much because I didn't have much money.

I had been used to being a waitress serving people and I was not used to being waited on.

What money I did have went to the house and my children.

Entertainment revolved around activities for my children rather than adult activities.

I felt like I was in a scene from the film Pretty Woman with the slippery suckers as a dish.

To be fair, I felt comfortable around his friends and we all chatted and got on well.

Halfway through the meal I decided to go outside for a cigarette break.

As I started smoking, a man came up to me and asked for a light.

Suddenly out from nowhere as I looked at him I could feel all his pain and anguish inside of him.

My psychic abilities were being called into action like a super hero, although I am not super or a hero; I am just me.

I started to give this man a reading and we sat in his car because it was more private.

I forgot the time as I was focused on helping this man.

Suddenly my partner came outside as he had wondered were I was and saw me in this man's car.

He knocked on the window of the car and this made the reading come to an abrupt stop.

I got out of the car and my half boyfriend started to moan at me for being so rude and going off like that without letting them know what I was doing.

I had been so used to this happening when I was out with my ex-husband who understood my work, that I came down to reality with a bump.

I was gutted for so many different reasons as my heart was in the right place. All I was doing was helping someone. My work isn't always a nine to five job and actually I am on call any time of the day.

I was hurt for being told off. My crime was only that I cared about someone even if that someone was a physical stranger, because to my soul they were not strangers at all.

I realized I would not have the same understanding and support about my psychic side with him as I had with my ex-husband.

My heart started to feel heavy as this made me realize what a soul connection that I had with him, compared to the physical connection that I had with this part-time boyfriend.

I decided to keep this side of myself to myself from now on when I was out with him.

Love can really hurt sometimes even when your intentions come from a place of love.

This took me back to when I was fourteen years old when I would go and visit an old lady from the church.

She was lonely and so I would go round to see her and we would chat about the old times and the war and she would show me her photo albums.

She only lived around the corner so she was within walking distance.

I knew I had to be home by half nine because I had school the next morning.

I kept saying to this old lady, "I have got to go otherwise I would be late for home."

She kept talking and would not listen to me and so I was late.

I got told off by my foster parents although I explained to them the reason for me being late, which made no difference.

They had called the old lady up asking her why I was late and the old lady blamed it on me.

I was fuming that I had selflessly given my time and love to this old lady, only to get in trouble for it.

Needless to say I never went round there again.

I didn't' want to be around people who took advantage of my kindness, love, and care.

I had to have some boundaries.

Why was it so hard for people to recognize an action of kindness? Why couldn't they make allowances if an action helped someone in need of help?

I just didn't feel it was fair that I got told off for caring about someone.

My guard around my psychic abilities was now up; I didn't feel comfortable enough to let myself go around my part-time boyfriend.

I couldn't wait to get home as I had ruined the evening.

I said I was sorry and gave up trying to explain that this is what happens in my kind of work.

Being psychic makes life unpredictable.

You never know when you are needed as it is my heart that pulls me to work, not my mind.

The experience reminded me that I was not free to do my work when it was required of me, yet I had to accept that people would intrude in our evening for his autograph and it all seemed one-sided to me.

A few months later my part-time boyfriend invited me to a family BBQ.

It was the first time that I would meet his brothers and sister.

I got talking to his sister-in-law who was lovely and very open; she made me feel comfortable enough to share my psychic side.

We exchanged phone numbers at the end of the evening and stayed in touch.

One day my part-time boyfriend called me to say how concerned he was about his brother and that his sister-in-law wondered if I would do a reading to help them.

I said, "Of course. No problem."

His sister-in-law called me and I tuned in and passed on what I was being shown.

This helped them and so their concern was now over.

I was thankful that he had a chance to see how readings help support people in a crisis or if they need reassurance and confirmation.

He slowly came round to the idea of what I did and didn't give me such a hard time about it after that.

I could not help that I had been born like this.

It was just part of who I am.

I was invited to an important function in the celebrity world. It was a sit down meal at a posh hotel in London.

I sat at a big round table with many cast members from his show.

I got asked what I did and so I said that I was a psychic medium.

I didn't want to say that I was just a mum.

I thought that my reply would be the end of the discussion.

During the break between eating and speeches many people from my table, came up to me wanting me to give them a mini reading.

I got on well with them and didn't feel out of my depth.

I was relieved that I didn't stick out like a sore thumb, and because his cast friends got on with me this made my part-time boyfriend happy.

I was thankful for the experiences I had with him.

I decided that I wanted to get another tattoo to cover up the whip mark scars on my back. This abuse happened after my mum died and I share this in my first book *From Both Sides of The Fence, The Gifts in U.*

I got my daughter to design a tattoo, a love heart in the design of wings.

My part-time boyfriend wanted a tattoo too.

He arranged a late night slot at his friend's shop.

We both got our tattoos and I was so thankful that this covered up my scars, as I wanted to cover them with some tender loving care.

You could say I wanted to give myself some love, and I wanted my love towards my self to be seen.

At least people would hopefully see the love heart rather than my scars, as I didn't want to be asked about them when they got noticed.

After this event I didn't get asked to attend anything as his girlfriend, instead I was asked as just a friend because he no longer needed me.

I was a part-time girlfriend behind closed doors.

I did not feel safe in this situation and I didn't appreciate being flavour of the month one minute then discarded when I was no longer needed.

I found our relationship becoming less fun with more arguments; this resulted in our relationship becoming more of an exchange through the phone.

I wasn't happy and didn't feel like I had a valuable place in his life.

This relationship was my biggest head fuck that I had experienced so far, and yet an eye-opener.

I always gave people a chance and it takes a lot for me to give up on someone, especially if I see a glimmer of depth and meaning.

I tended to put all my energy into people, even if it was a detriment to myself.

I was taught that everyone comes first before your self. This was something the vicar had told me.

This was the worst advice I had ever listened to as it sent me up dead ends and losing sight of myself.

Luckily my soul is my real guide and always got me back on track, no matter how many times I fell.

I had met many different people while connecting with the actor.

He opened my eyes to things that I would have been closed off from on my path otherwise.

I was always thankful of understanding more.

I met people that cross-dressed and those that where transitioning.

I felt respect towards them for being brave enough to wear their truth as well as be it, rather than hide.

I saw their sadness at how they had to go through the back doors instead of the front.

I saw how they wished they had the freedom to be themselves like anyone else.

Really is it about gender, as we don't go around looking under people's clothing to see what sexual organs they have.

We have to rely on dress sense, colour codes and make up as clues.

It seems to me what everyone is really fighting over is some space to be themselves without other people getting in their way.

The truth is that everyone has access to infinite space; that is in the soul.

We forget because we believe what we see as our material space as the only space that we have.

When you switch from the physical space to your soul space you feel free and light without the burden of the physical getting in your way.

When you live from your soul space, other souls respect it, but if it is shone through the physical like shining a light through a physical room then the physical side sees the room not the light of your soul.

If you walk past a house in the dark of night and you see that a light is on, you may be drawn to look in the window. You look to see what is in the room, not the light itself.

This example explains this well.

If you see just a bright light you notice the light and nothing else.

How you reflect your soul is your own choice and responsibility.

It depends how you wish to be seen, in total clarity or in distortion.

Equally how you master the physical is a choice, to live a life in limitation or expansion.

Meanwhile when I met up with my ex-husband he didn't seem himself.

He seemed really sad and not well.

His sister passing hit him hard and brought back memories of loss rather than gain.

He missed living and being married to me, yet something inside me just would not let me go back.

It was nothing personal towards him, as I loved him.

It is something that confused me too.

He had heart-burn and took tablets for it. He said, "I am sure I have a brain tumor or something."

I said, "If you're concerned go and see a doctor." I didn't ask him too many questions because I selfishly didn't want to think about him being unwell. Being such a rock in my life, I thought it was just a passing comment in conversation and nothing too serious to worry about.

Autumn was drawing in and I was getting ready for Halloween and bonfire night.

It was now that time of year to start getting ready and prepared for Christmas.

On my daughters birthday my ex-husband came round to give her a present once he finished work.

We spent more time together and I told him that I had a date for my operation to have my labiaplasty, on my vagina lips.

It was booked in for the beginning of January.

He said, "I had forgotten that you had gone to the doctors about that. I'm glad you have got a date and didn't have to wait too long."

I asked him if he would come with me, to which he replied, "Of course."

It was lovely that even in divorce we never lost each other; divorce hadn't changed us.

Every day we would keep in touch, either by phone or he would pop in to mine or I would pop into his.

We just could not be apart, only on paper.

I kept having a dream where I was going down for surgery and my ex-husband is by my side and I know I won't make it through the surgery. I kept trying to tell him that I know I am going to die during surgery and would he tell my kids how much I love them.

It was like he wasn't listening to me or taking me seriously and he just smiled.

I was so convinced that this was my looming fate that I wrote goodbye letters to my children.

I told him what songs I wanted at my funeral and had become at peace with my passing.

Everyone around me thought I was losing the plot and just humored me.

I loved that we are there for each other not because of a bit of paper but because of the love that we shared.

186

We faced life together no matter how ugly or painful it got.

His children accepted our relationship and understood the bond that we had.

I appreciated that we all were on the same page without judgment.

I love his children while being respectful of my place, I trusted they knew where I was if they ever needed a friend.

While round his flat I told him that the film King Kong was out the following week, and would he like to go and see it?

He said, "Yes, of course." I had brought with me a Christmas present that I wanted to give to him early. I felt he would find them useful, as the weather was getting colder.

They were some warm socks for work. Not very exciting but at least practical and he said he was thankful of them.

I would give him his other gifts on the day.

I noticed he seemed there but not. There was something different about him as if he was in his own little world.

I brushed the thought to one side and thought it must be just a passing phase.

He asked me to give him a quick reading, as he wanted to know if his life would change next year. I said he would feel more settled next year.

The next day while I sat in my lounge, a huge angel appeared in front of me.

I liked all my fairy ornaments that my children had bought me, but I wasn't really into angels nor did I know anything about them. I just thought they were a myth or some magical tale.

As I looked at him I felt puzzled as he looked nothing like the angels that were depicted or that had been drawn.

I say a he as he looked like a man going by his masculine build, and nothing to do with sexual gender. His energy felt strong too.

His wings were huge and when I say huge they took up the length of my lounge wall.

It was funny although he was taller than my lounge the ceiling didn't get in his way.

His wings were not white and flat like bird feathers.

They were bulbous and thick wings and they looked heavy with black veins running through the sepia ivory looking colour of each wing.

I asked him how he managed to carry such heavy looking wings.

He explained to me that they weren't heavy, that they are light like a canoe.

I said ok as this made sense to me.

I also asked how he moved about with such big cumbersome wings.

He showed me how they folded flat to his body.

He then showed me were he was from.

I saw a landscape so green with lots of water and waterfalls. I had never seen such a beautiful place before.

The leaves on the trees were so big, something I would imagine you would see in the Amazon Jungle.

He picked up a water lily and showed me how they use them to see their reflection like we use mirrors.

I held it in my hand and it felt thick and waxy; I looked at my reflection as I bent my head to look in it.

Drops of water still lay fresh on the leaf where he had picked it up out of the lake.

In the distance I saw a big hill with someone standing wearing white clothing.

The angel handed me a very tiny envelope and said it was a message. I didn't know what was in the envelope.

I immediately thought it was a message for my ex-husband as he had asked for a reading.

I didn't think it was a message for me.

It was the last thing on my mind.

As the angel went he had left me with an excitement that I had never felt before.

I wanted to know if there was anything written about angels in the library.

I rushed out the house curious to find out.

I found a book all about the different types of angels.

I wanted to know if an angel associated with water would be in this book.

I could not believe my eyes as I read that Angel Gabriel represents the flowing element of water.

So it is true that I had seen the real Angel Gabriel.

It is something I will never forget, his vision as clear to me as the day he visited.

I didn't understand why he had visited me and what the message in the letter was all about, but I trusted one day it would make sense.

The vision of him and how he looked over shone the tiny envelope anyway.

I was struck how dull his wings looked in colour and not shining bright white.

I thought if artists had seen how he really looked it would be a mix of Hercules in stature and wings as bulbous like a canoe.

Not delicate and light as portrayed.

He looks solid and as strong as an ox.

I knew no one would believe me that I had been visited by him, only those who have an open mind, so I just shared it with my family and those I trusted.

It was handy that I wasn't physically knowledgeable; my soul would show me things my physical side would not know.

I knew and those that knew me, knew, that I would literally not be able to make it up even if I had wanted to.

I was busy with a hectic life and didn't have enough time on my hands to be bored enough to make stuff up so my life would be more interesting.

This is where the library and later search engines on the computer came in handy.

I would search to see if anything matched what I knew.

The following week my ex-husband picked me up to watch the film King Kong.

He bought our tickets while I bought our snacks.

We took our seats and he sat on the right side of me.

I looked at him halfway through because of a sad part in the film.

Usually he would have responded and looked at me back. He would have been aware of me looking at him.

Today he looked straight ahead as if I wasn't there.

He looked so different and odd as if there but not.

I brushed it off and just thought he was having an off day.

He had no emotion and just watched the film with a blank expression on his face.

This was not like him.

The film ended and he kindly drove me home and we kissed each other goodnight. People can be off or different for many reasons and I knew him well enough that if he wanted to share something, he would.

As I walked through the door I forgot to check the lottery and I texted him to send me the numbers and he did when he got home.

The next morning I was busy doing some housework, my children had broken up from school for the Christmas holidays.

My phone rang at twelve- midday and my ex-husband's second eldest was on the other end of the line.

She told me that my ex-husband her dad had collapsed at work and had died.

My body slid down my wall while I screamed down the phone, "NOOOOOO!"

My children came running over, as they had never heard such a sound come from me.

I told them that he had died.

My eldest took the phone off me, as I was unable to speak.

The light of my life had just gone out.

I spoke to his children later in the day when I was able to speak.

Three days before Christmas, being jolly was the last thing on my mind.

I went to see him at the hospital. He was on a bed with wheels that went along a track.

He was behind a window so I could not even touch him.

He had a post mortem and it came back that he had a heart attack and had lung disease, which explained his long-term cough.

We shared what we had noticed different about him leading up to his passing and how he had written down his contact numbers from his phone onto a pad of paper in his lounge.

This helped his children to contact people to let them know.

His funeral arrangements were made for the beginning of January.

My operation was booked in for five days before his funeral.

Christmas came and went like a blur; we all put on a brave face and made it as happy as we could.

A part of me was angry with him for going on this particular day.

What are the odds of him passing, when my mother did on the same date!

December would now be a doubly painful month for me, both passing suddenly over night.

I felt for his children.

It was like life around us was in slow motion.

I felt numb and totally lost without him.

We did everything together.

With Christmas out of the way, the New Year started off with my operation.

My daughter drove me to the hospital as a day patient.

We arrived early and after a couple of hours a doctor checked me over and I was then wheeled down to the operating theatre.

All I kept thinking about was my dream and wondered what side I would wake up.

The operation was a success and a short while later I was wheeled out of the recovery room to a ward.

Seeing my daughter was such a relief as I had been convinced I was going to die.

What I was being prepared for was my ex-husband passing not me, I just didn't understand the message.

Back home I had about five days to heal before the funeral.

This gave me enough time to be able to walk more comfortably.

I am glad I had the operation but nothing could have prepared me for it.

It was more painful than giving birth.

Maybe it was because I had so many stitches that I had not experienced after having children.

The day of the funeral came and word had got back to the foster family that he had passed.

I told them I did not want them to come to his funeral, as we had not seen each other for some time.

They didn't respect my wishes and turned up anyway, I was polite and that was about it, but deep down inside I just thought, *Why could you not think about the wishes of someone else rather than your own?*

You just cannot control people. They will do what they wish to do.

My youngest daughter's father turned up which was a great support.

My daughters came, but I felt my youngest was too young and selfishly my decision for her not to come to the funeral were for my own selfish reasons.

I just didn't feel that I would be able to put on a brave face for her.

I had a big enough challenge holding myself up.

The funeral celebrated him with such love and respect.

After the funeral we stayed in touch with his children.

This faded as the months and time went on, not because I didn't want to be there for them, I just didn't want to tread on their mums toes or be a burden to them.

I didn't know what his children wanted and hoped they knew us well enough to know that our door was always open. I told them that if they needed us, we always would be there.

The first three months, I stayed in my bedroom mourning him.

I could not function. My whole world came crashing down.

I didn't know how to start living and doing things on my own as I had been so used to us being together.

Even going up into the loft felt odd, as he had always done it.

My life caught up with me, my past crashed into me, I spiraled into a breakdown and melt down.

I was thankful for my youngest daughter's dad supporting me as he had his daughter a lot so I would have time to heal.

I was a mess and in a dark place.

I started to drink as soon as I woke up and not just in the evening, to numb the pain.

I was losing my grip on life and felt like everything was falling through my fingers.

My children would argue and I did not handle it as well as I had previously because I felt my pain not just of the present but to do with my past was making me fall apart at my seams.

I was at breaking point so bad and one day my children pushed me too far.

I had tried so hard to keep myself at bay from them.

They started and I don't know what possessed me but I took a knife from the kitchen and marched upstairs to their bedroom in a rage.

I flew through their bedroom door and started screaming at my two eldest daughters at the top of my voice.

I shouted, "Are you trying to kill me off? Well here I will make it easy for you!" and I told them to stab me as I held out the knife to them.

I totally lost my shit.

After I had let off steam and finally blew my top, I calmed down and felt awful for doing such a scary thing in front of them.

As I went over what had happened, I had a flashback of my mother holding a knife too, so it must have been something that I had witnessed with her.

But she had an excuse. She had a mental illness. I didn't, I just had a broken heart mind and body.

I remembered back to how the foster family tried to change me into a perfect daughter to match their own, how the tutor teaching me how to speak proper gave up on me too.

I had always been the black sheep, the one who didn't get top marks. Every year at school I would be put in the dunce class, destined to always be a dunce.

I would never amount to anything much, an invisible outcast in the world, but it didn't have to be like this for my girls.

I tried to keep my shit together but every now and then as the children grew, if I felt out of control I would not always react very well.

It is not that I meant to ever deliberately hurt my children. It was a cry for help at times. Luckily, I did have friends who understood and I could talk to them and I was able to work through the situations that came up.

They were just kids and saw me as a strong mum but I was still human and at that time, life was too much.

I am not super woman but at times I wish I could have been.

I was just me, trying to hold my pain in and keep my head above water.

I remembered back to when they were young and how I would write down to-do lists to try and be a perfect mum.

I used to collapse in floods of tears if I had not completed my to-do mother list. I would feel like I had let them all down.

In hindsight, I bet my girls where none the wiser. I had set myself such high standards of what I thought a mum should be like, standards so high that I could not even rise to them.

I tried my best to be perfect but everywhere I looked whether it was at my past or the present all I could see was what a failure I was.

The only thing I had left to offer my children is that I was still here and that's it.

The thought had crossed my mind for five minutes, would they be better off being in care themselves?

As I just did not feel good enough for them.

This thought left me as soon as it came.

I reminded myself how lucky I was to have such amazing daughters and that I have them as my reason to live and get up every day.

I did not want to have to rely on drink to get me through the day, so I tipped what drink I had left in the bottle down the sink.

Something switched in me. I suddenly looked at myself and thought, *Enough is enough. Tomorrow is a new day.*

I can't give up. I have four daughters that need me, I need to sort myself out and get back on my feet.

The first thing that I did was get up in to the loft, as silly as this sounds it was my first thing that I could do that was within easy access.

I then faced all the other things that I would have to do on my own.

In the week I decided to drive to a local food shop, one that we would often go to together.

I got lost and ended up miles away and didn't know how to get home.

In a panic I called my youngest daughter's dad who guided me home by giving his daughter directions to pass on to me.

Day by day I got stronger and back on my feet.

I could not believe that although we where divorced on paper, in our hearts we were not, and so to me at thirty-eight-years-old, I was now a widow.

A few weeks later I was lying in bed and just drifting off to sleep, I heard his voice as clear as day say to me, "Go for it. Now it's your time."

I didn't understand his message fully, but it was so lovely to hear his voice and to know that he was ok.

I felt like he was giving me his blessing and encouragement to continue with my life even though it felt like I was facing the unknown.

He had become the only family that I had, apart from my children, whom I trusted and felt safe with.

I will always be thankful to my husband that passed and for all he brought to my and my children's life. He saw what I thought was missing in me and showed me it was there all along.

He said to me, "What's the matter with you?" I shrugged my shoulders and he said, "NOTHING."

This one sentence I held onto and it has been my lifeline.

He didn't see me as my shitty past. He saw the gold inside of me, my real worth.

In death he encouraged me to face myself.

At first it was tough as it meant I had to go back to come forward.

I decided to go back over my childhood history.

I went into the loft to find my folders from being in the care system.

There were blank areas with no information.

I decided to use my psychic abilities to retrieve my past.

I hated the child in me as much as I hated my childhood.

I went back to the scene of when I was abused and whipped.

As I tuned into my past I saw my childhood abuser.

He had a mustache and small beard around his mouth and smelt of cigarettes and beer.

The scene of the sexual abuse unfolded but all I saw was the pain in his face.

As I visited the past I knew I was free and did not have to be stuck in the past.

I just needed to know why and understand why he did it.

Visiting it, I got my answer and was shown how it was not about me at all; it was all about him.

He was taking out his pain, his frustrations, and own insecurities all out on me, I just happened to be in the same place and space as him.

Once I found my answer, I felt at peace with the abuse and didn't feel a victim and I felt sorry for him and I was ok.

I saw how I was physically abused with a stick, which caused me to have a weak back from the injuries, something I learned to live with.

I saw and felt how he only had access to my flesh but not my soul as my soul left my body and watched the scene as I am doing now.

I was free from the abuse; my skin took the brunt, which left its mark.

I remember how one night I got out of bed, unable to cope with any more pain.

I walked out of my backdoor barefoot with my nightgown on.

I collapsed on to my hands and knees sobbing with tears falling down my cheeks.

I cried out for mercy, begging for the pain in my life to stop.

I could not take another day and just wanted my life to end.

I had done nearly forty years of facing adversity, when was life going to give me a break?

At this point I was not scared of dying as I had lived with death all my life.

I felt like I had nothing left to give, life had been sucked out of me.

Hitting rock bottom is horrible and unless you have been there, you won't know what it feels like.

I felt like I was in a hole that was so deep and I didn't see a way out of it.

I didn't know how to face my future although I had faced my past.

I had cried so many feelings over so many months that I felt like I would never be able to cry ever again.

I remembered the words my ex-husband said to me. "Please promise me you will write your book." I said I would.

I didn't feel it would be the world beyond book I had half started.

The following day, my friend called me up to say she felt she had something to tell me.

She said, "I feel you should go to college."

I replied, "No, I am not feeling that."

But the thought had been planted.

I continued to see my actor boyfriend once a month until we both decided a year later that we wanted different things in life.

We went our different ways and parted kindly and wished each other well for the future.

The seed that had previously been planted about going to college had resurfaced.

I decided to enroll at my local college to do an Indian Head Massage course.

I chose this course because my guide was a North American Indian; the word Indian had sold it to me.

I had been told as a child that I was uneducable, so I wanted to go back to college to see if this label was true.

And so the next chapter of my life begins.

OVERVIEW

Looking back it now made sense why I was unable to settle in my last marriage.

It confused me so much while I was going through it because we had not fallen out of love.

They say things happen for a reason and the reason why things turned out the way they did in our case, I believe, was so his children had a chance to spend some quality time with him without us getting in the way. This is something I am thankful for, for them.

They had fun experiences together and made many happy memories.

No one missed out during those two years of change.

As much as the flesh is buried, the essence of who we are continues.

He will always have a place in our family as he does with his own family for sure.

A few months later, I started to go through some paperwork, and came across my parents death certificates.

I was shocked to read that my mum had passed away on the 20th December and not the 22nd December as I had thought. I had said this date since I met him and wondered if it was because I had seen his death date in him all along.

This would make more sense to why I felt our marriage had to end physically speaking.

In some ways finding out this information gave me some comfort that things turned out just how they should be.

I had experienced so many angles of love so far, from relationships of situation and circumstance to escaping the past.

To have been married and divorced three times by the age of thirty-eight, with four daughters would be viewed by some as damaged goods.

I had been told in an argument once, "Who would want you with four children?"

I never saw my colourful life as damaged; I saw how much experience I had so far.

I didn't see loss, only gain.

My relationships came to an end for different reasons, but I never walked away empty handed.

Two relationships gave me the gift of my daughters.

One relationship reunited me with my mother's ashes.

The other relationship introduced me to a relationship past the physical flesh and bones, a relationship deeper than a beating heart. It was the connection of two souls.

The relationship I had with the actor encouraged me to face myself and unlock the block I had put on my past, like a padlock without a key.

I listened to him because we both came from the children's homes, something we both related to.

My experiences with my daughters taught me how to forgive myself; they may have seen the ugly side of me but they always focused on the love in me that I shared, rather than my inadequacies.

I was thankful to my foster home for making space for me to physically grow. I appreciated that they gave their best to a child that had a lot of love to give but the pain inside just overflowed.

I wished them well but I was unable to find myself in their place they called home. It was no one's fault and just how it was.

It was never just bad; we had fun times too and brought to the table what we all needed.

Looking back, all my relationships were a vital piece that helped me to get to where I am now.

It wasn't easy. It was exhausting and a challenge and often pushed me to my limits.

I was sick of being in pain year in year out.

People may look at my track record and think, *Wow. Why can't she hold down a relationship?*

There must be something wrong with her if she has been married so many times and failed.

She must be hard work.

No matter how you view it or judge it, or what label you stick on it, or how you opinionate over it, the reason is known not at face value. The meaning can be found when you piece your life together. If you look at it separately, it won't make much sense.

I could have dwelled on loss and mourning and death.

I could have focused on being a victim.

I could have been stuck in feeling a failure.

I could have given up after the life I've had so far.

I could have turned to drugs of any kind and committed suicide and meant it.

I turned to alcohol and different substances as a crutch, knowing I would be a slave to it, thinking that I was not enough on my own.

I knew no one would drag me out of my life and that it was down to me to get my shit together.

I wanted my children to be proud of me as much as I am of them.

I had some decisions to make, on how I evaluated myself.

Did I listen to what people had told me who had crossed my path or did I start listening to myself and empowering myself?

I knew that if I finally wanted to settle in life, I first had to be settled in myself, which I hadn't been able to do up until now.

I had felt like I had always been on the run from life as well as from myself.

I had to stop running now.

I had faced my past and got enough answers that I needed to feel at peace with my history.

I accepted that sometimes there are no answers, and that's ok.

I didn't want to get obsessed with my past either.

I knew I had to put as much effort in myself as I did others.

It was time to give some energy back to myself.

No one is equipped to judge anyone especially if you have not walked in that persons shoes.

It would be like me judging how to cut hair when I don't do it for a living or even a hobby.

The most important thing I realized from this chapter of my life is about loving myself. Otherwise I was constantly chasing after love that I felt was missing inside.

Realizing this, I came to a decision that I needed some time out from personal relationships.

I was not interested in having any more relationships and would concentrate on it just being us girls.

CHAPTER SEVEN

39- PRESENT DAY

I started college at the beginning of September.

I had picked up my uniform, which looked very professional and explained what type of course that I had enrolled in.

I was in two minds about doing this course because the tutor who had interviewed me explained that the whole course would be done by using a computer, rather than handwritten, as they had changed it this year.

This sent me into a meltdown. She also said this course was a diploma course and quite intense.

I had only chosen this course by the name Indian. I also just wanted to know if I could be educated.

I personally didn't have a computer and really didn't know what to do, as the children where using the one they had.

I felt like I had been dragged to the interview by one of my ears by my guide, and felt I should turn up and face my educational fears.

Even if I had a computer I didn't know how to use one. I felt out of my depth and overwhelmed. This didn't feel a good start and felt like everything was against me to put me off.

A friend bought me a computer and I agreed to pay them back.

Another friend set it all up for me.

I asked my daughters to show me the basics around it.

It was a mad rush of panic, but thanks to my friends, I was able to turn up and start the course.

It was one evening a week for three hours. Many women showed up to the course.

We all introduced ourselves and the tutor explained the modules involved.

It felt good doing something for myself.

My children where supportive and they gave me the space I needed.

A couple of weeks in, a new face turned up at college. It was a male student.

I thought he was brave turning up for a class full of women.

He fitted in well and didn't seam fazed by us.

My eldest two daughters had left school and started college also, so they knew the level of commitment needed to do the course work.

My second oldest daughter didn't complete her college course and left to get a job.

My third daughter was having bullying issues at senior school, and so she left to start college part-time.

They cannot deal with the bullies so they encouraged my daughter to leave. They chose to remove the victim. Go figure! And you wonder why the school system is outdated.

She actually enjoyed the course and enjoyed the change of scene although leaving school without any qualifications and missing out on the prom was harsh.

I held her hand and told her, "Life is unfair at times but look for the benefits this situation is opening up for you. You can take any exams at college it is only a different building, that's all.

And you will find that you will mix with more mature people.

Concentrate on you and what you want to achieve. Don't let school stop you or put you off."

I went on to say how many famous actors had left school with nothing and it didn't stop them from having a career.

You can be taught many things in a moment but experience stays a lifetime.

She was brave and faced her path that was opening up for her with dignity and not fear.

She may have felt scared but this is not the same as fear.

My youngest was at junior school and enjoying expressing herself.

She had met some lovely friends. One day she decided that she didn't want to wear girl's clothes and so I respected her wishes and got her some boy boxers and pants, and trousers.

Her close friend wore the same. She was what you would describe as a tomboy rather than a princess.

I got the vibe it would be a passing phase and I respected she knew what she wanted. I thought, *Its only clothes. What harm can they do?*

Once she had got it out of her system, she went back to wearing skirts and knickers.

At college I made friends with the male in the class as he made me laugh.

If we got put together, all you could hear was giggling as we took turns massaging each other's heads.

I don't know how the tutor had patience with us, as we didn't stifle our giggles.

The course work took many hours to complete taking up any spare time that I had.

We would meet up and practice our massage routines on one another.

He started to pick me up for college to save me walking during the winter months.

Often we had not eaten before college had started, so we would buy a portion of chips after and eat them in his car before he dropped me off home.

It was nice having a friend to share the college work with.

I would practice my Indian head massage routine on my children and they never complained.

It was time for us to take our practical exam. I had previously already handed in my course work, so I knew this had been marked.

I was nervous because this was more than just a college course to me. It would tell me if I was educable or not.

As we entered the classroom we all took our places ready to do the exam.

The tutor observed our every move.

Finally the exam was over and we all sat down and waited to be called by the tutor, one by one to be given our results.

My name was called and I slowly walked over to her desk to sit down, anticipating my results.

The tutor told me that I had passed with distinction.

I had tears in my eyes with pure relief and joy.

I was proud that I had passed with flying colours, but I was equally pleased that I was not the label that had been given to me as a child.

I was so happy that I faced my fears so I could face my truth of who I really am.

It is easy to dish out labels but when they stick it is hard to let go of them.

Everyone on our course passed. With smiling faces, we arranged to meet up for a leaving meal.

I wanted to go of course, but I could not afford it as all my money went on my children with the costs of running a home.

The older they got, my money went down not up.

My male friend from college asked me if I was going to go to the meal. I said, "No because I can't afford it."

He said, "Oh please come. You can't miss it. I will pay for your meal for you."

I said, "Really thank you but I feel bad you doing that for me."

He said, "No not at all. I don't want you missing the meal."

As he dropped me off I could see my children's faces peering out of the lounge window waiting for me to arrive home.

They knew I would be getting my results.

I said goodbye to my friend and ran to our front door.

My daughters all asked me at once how I got on.

I smiled the biggest grin and said, "I passed with distinction!" We had the biggest group hug.

My daughters started to tease me and said, the man at college seems nice, always picking you up and dropping you home.

"I think he likes you, mum. You should go out with him."

I said, "No, it's nothing like that. We just get on well and are friends I have had no vibes from him to tell me that he likes me.

I am not looking for a relationship any way."

"Mum, we are all growing up and we don't want you to be on your own."

Those words really touched my heart that my daughters had been thinking about my future and life.

I thought they were too busy with their own lives to think about mine.

It made me happy to know that they would not mind sharing me again as we had been on our own for a little while.

The man from college was nothing more than a friend. It did make me wonder why everyone kept thinking there was more to our friendship.

Even the other women in our class thought there was more to our friendship. Being friendly doesn't always mean flirting. It made me feel cross with the assumption. because in my head we were innocently being friends. Why does sex have to come into it just because we get on and have a laugh and spend time together?

Male and females can be just friends without benefits.

Being the open person that I am, I told him what people were saying including my daughters.

I told him how I was genuinely puzzled why people thought this.

He just brushed it off and was not bothered about it.

A couple of weeks later he picked me up for our college leaving meal.

It was an evening full of chatting and laughter.

Our tutor asked us if we were going to do any more courses.

A few of us from our class had decided to go on to do a reflexology course.

I said I would enroll during the summer holidays.

As the meal came to a close my tutor got the bill and worked out how much we all would need to put in.

We split the bill between us and my friend settled mine for me. I was thankful and told him so as we all said our goodbyes after exchanging telephone numbers.

My male friend offered to give me a lift home.

As he pulled up outside my house he leant over to kiss me, which I responded.

He said he had wanted to ask me out for ages but wanted to get the course out the way first.

I said, "Did you? I had no idea that you liked me. I am shocked. You gave nothing away."

We became boyfriend and girlfriend there and then.

I told my girls that the man from college had asked me out, and that I had agreed to go out with him.

My girls all laughed and said, "See Mum? We knew he liked you!"

I don't know how everyone saw what I didn't see.

My boyfriend got to know my girls and came round for dinner from time to time.

I would see him at his flat too.

We both enrolled to do the reflexology course.

It didn't start until September so we had a couple of months off.

My 40th birthday was fast approaching and my eldest daughter had a good job working in retail and wanted to get me something special.

She decided that she wanted to get me a new sofa; as I had only ever had second hand ones.

She sent me pictures on my phone of sofas that she had seen.

She bought me one and I could not wait. I was so excited that it would be here in time for my birthday.

She said, "Mum, I never see you sit down and relax. You sit on the floor with your boots on."

When the new sofa arrived, I made a conscious effort to take my boots off and sit down on the sofa.

I even traded in my boots for wearing slippers.

My fortieth birthday was so much fun. I decided to go to a theme park with my family. My daughters spoilt me and we had professional pictures done of us together to mark my fortieth.

What a change a decade makes! On my thirtieth, I was alone with just my daughters.

My boyfriend didn't come with us because he was afraid of rides.

The dynamics of my family were changing.

My daughters adapted to sharing me with my boyfriend.

My eldest daughter was enjoying her job working in a clothing shop.

At Christmas my third daughter started going out with a boy from a different country and he asked her out on Christmas day.

My second oldest daughter was quite happy being single, as she had not long finished a relationship.

My youngest was eight going on nine and she was happy doing her own thing. She didn't mind her own company, as she was laid back and chilled in character.

Our tutor for our reflexology course was nothing like our last tutor that we had for Indian head.

We had been spoilt with our last tutor that was for sure.

The quality was missing and it taught me that you can learn and memorize a subject but it doesn't mean you know it and fully understand it.

My boyfriend had booked a holiday to go to Canada on a whale-watching trip.

He had gone many times before, travelling around Canada for six months on his own.

His mate had offered to drop him off to the airport and didn't mind me tagging along to see him off.

I had one too many drinks at the airport bar and got a bit emotional when it was time for my boyfriend to leave to board the plane.

I knew I would be left with his mate that I didn't know very well as I had only been going out with my boyfriend four months.

His mate got me one more drink and he could see that I was upset and he so pulled me onto his lap.

Out of nowhere he started to kiss me and I froze not knowing what to do.

Once he had finished I got off from his lap and started to drink my drink.

I felt awkward and could not wait to get home.

We decided to stop off to get some chips to eat in the car on the way home.

The drive could not finish quick enough for me.

I felt like I had been kicked in the stomach.

I felt like history was repeating itself.

I was so upset and felt like I had betrayed my boyfriend before we had even had a start.

I could not even phone him to tell him what had happened.

I got myself into a right state. I didn't want his mate saying that I had tried it on with him when I hadn't.

My boyfriend was best man at his friend's wedding so he would believe him over me.

I then started to feel gutted for him. I didn't want him to lose his best friend, so I thought the best thing to do was to keep the incident to myself.

The stress of it made me ill, I went to the doctors and she told me to see a specialist. I was diagnosed with having Episcleritis of the eye. This is when the whites of your eye become red and sore. It is painful to look down.

I was given steroid drops that I had to put in my eye for two weeks.

I was told that it was not curable and they didn't know the cause.

I wondered if it was because I had worn contact lenses since I was sixteen years old.

I was unable to wear my contacts until my eye cleared up.

It was something like herpes that once you have it you always have it.

I was told if it flares up again to go straight to hospital for the eye drops.

Holding this secret of what happened at the airport left me with a horrible feeling inside.

My boyfriend came home from his trip and all I could think about was if I should tell him or not.

It didn't bother me if it meant I would lose my boyfriend by telling the truth, what I couldn't live with was ruing his friendship with his mate.

I was in such a dilemma and the longer that time passed, the harder it got.

College kept my mind busy, although we were not enjoying our reflexology course but we decided to continue with it. At least we would come out of it with another qualification to our names.

It was nice catching up with some of the women from our last class.

They where pleased to hear our news about being boyfriend and girlfriend.

The next half term, my boyfriend bought tickets to take my youngest and myself to visit the LONDON ZOO. I thought it was nice of him to buy the tickets but deep down I was not too keen on seeing animals behind bars and cages. It just didn't sit with my heart. I prefer to know they are roaming in the wild in their natural habitat.

My daughter enjoyed herself and our first day trip out.

I spent the next couple of months sorting out my youngest daughter's birthday and getting ready for Christmas. This year I had a boyfriend to buy presents for to add to my list. I love Christmas and would put all my heart and soul into making it as a magical as I could.

My boyfriend came round with a surprise for my girls as an early joint Christmas present for them. We were all intrigued with the big boxes that he carried through our front door. It was a computer. Wow! What a big gift. My daughters here over the moon as our last computer had a number of things wrong with it being old in computer terms. My girls gathered round him so they could set up the computer together. I could not believe he got this for them.

It was getting close to Christmas Day and we realized that we didn't have enough chairs for everyone to sit at the table. We rushed to Ikea to get the amount of chairs that we would need. We sat down in the Ikea canteen for a coffee and a bite to eat.

Suddenly my boyfriend got down on one knee and asked me to marry him.

I said yes as we got on so well and my children loved him. He didn't have a ring as he just felt it and did it on the spur.

With just two days until Christmas Day, it made a change to have something to celebrate rather than to mourn. We left Ikea and rushed to the shops to get an engagement ring. When we got home, we broke the news to my girls.

My girls were so happy and welcomed him into our family unit. His family was happy for him too.

It may seem quick as we had only been going out for six months officially, but to us we had known each other for eighteen months and had already got to know each other first as friends. It's not like we were young. We were in our forties, so what was the point in waiting if you know?

I had awkward moments in those first months, as he reminded me of my ex-husband who had passed away. He had a similar vibe to him and was also very laid back.

They were so similar in character that even my daughters would comment on it.

I kept calling my fiancé by my ex-husband's name. It was a compliment. Luckily he understood and didn't take it personally.

Christmas Day felt extra magical it is the happiest I had been in a long time. My third daughter officially got asked to be her partner's girlfriend. My family was expanding and it wasn't just us girls anymore. Even our year old chi dog was female.

My fiancé now had a lot of women in his life. I felt so proud that two of my daughter's had past the age of eighteen and still wanted to know me. I was relieved that what their dad had said about them growing up to hate me had not come true yet.

As a family, we were looking forward to the New Year after the exciting end to this last one. It made me think about what I had thought to myself in my bedroom in the foster home at fourteen years old. I remember saying to myself that the first forty years of my life would be tough but the second forty would be easier.

I was forty years old now and it looked like what I thought all those years ago turned out to be correct. If this year was anything to go by, then I could look forward at last rather than constantly back over my shoulder.

With New Year celebrations out of the way, we all settled in to our daily routines.

I continued to do my psychic readings as well as giving Indian head treatments for my growing number of clients.

My fiancé told me that he had booked us to go away on a skiing holiday for a week in a couple months time. I was taken aback as skiing was the last thing I had ever thought about doing. My girls said I should go and that they would hold down the fort at home while my youngest would stay at her dad's for the week. My fiancé's family was also going to meet us there and I was feeling out of my comfort zone. We would be flying to the ski resort while his family would drive.

My fiancé took me shopping to buy me the skiing clothes that I would need. The skiing trip arrived and we boarded the plane, reaching our destination in a couple of hours. We arrived at our hotel and found our room and we looked around while we waited for his family to join us. The layout was insane. You could ski down to the hotel. The food choices were unreal and they even had a bowling alley in the games room.

They all knew how to ski, but I had never been, so he made arrangements for me to have some skiing lessons. I was not feeling confident at all. I was totally shitting myself. We went and got our ski equipment and went out on the slopes. My fiancé had the patience of a saint. With skis on my feet I froze on a slight slope, as I was scared of moving backwards.

A whole hour I stood there saying I could not move. Eventually I got my head around the skis and could see why I needed the lessons. It was certainly an adventure and I felt lucky to be treated to such a lovely holiday but my nerves spoilt it for me.

Every morning I would wake up feeling sick and complaining I was sick with nerves.

Skiing is hard work and not a relaxing holiday. I got used to it but had been thrown in the deep end rather than being eased into it. This matched the story of my life, as it had always been all or nothing. It was decided one morning that we would use a different chair lift, which meant skiing down to where the ski school met.

It had been snowing the night before and had been extra cold so the snow was extra frozen. We all got off the chair lift and stood in line ready to ski down the slope.

A couple of friends out of our group started to ski first and realized how frozen it was.

We had no other way of reaching the bottom and had no choice but to ski down.

I started to get really scared as I wasn't experienced enough to cope with these conditions. Two of the more experienced men at skiing in his family stood on either side of me to ski down this slope. With the snow so frozen and slick, we pushed off with our skis and we moved like bullets fired out of a gun. I squatted down on my skis. I thought if I were to fall, I would rather have less height as I would be closer to the floor. I didn't realize that this would make me go faster and the men grabbed each side of my jacket to support me down the slope.

When we reached the bottom I was thankful not to have fallen and I think they were thankful that the speed at which we went was over.

"Never again", I said. "I only want to use the gondola from now on."

We had hearty breakfasts that would fill our bellies for the day. I went to my skiing lesson in the afternoon, while my fiancé went with his family to ski the more advanced slopes. We all got on well and they all seemed friendly and approachable.

My fiancé would be waiting for me as my lesson finished at 5.30pm. We would ski back to the hotel and get washed and changed and ready for dinner.

We were starving and had built up an appetite. The food was as delicious as it looked.

We played a few games of bowling and had a hot chocolate brandy before bed. We went to bed early every night, as it was early starts to the day, so no lay in included in this trip. I called my girls to make sure they all were ok and I told them about my adventure.

The next day I didn't have any lessons booked so we decided to do our own thing.

We decided to do one complete run so I could say that I had achieved it before we left to go home. We got half way through the run when we took the next chair lift up to the top. The wind was picking up. We noticed there wasn't any staff manning at the bottom to help skiers off the lift. Our chair flew upwards into the air and my fiancé jumped off leaving me still on the chair. With his hand he grabbed my foot and pulled me off the chair. My hat flew off and I lost one of my skis. I nearly shit myself again and as I got to my feet and brushed myself down, my fiancé found my hat for me to place back on my head.

The chair behind us had a person that I recognized from my skiing class. She didn't manage to get off her chair and ended up going back round to where she came from.

We did manage to ski down the slope and the lifts were closed because of bad weather. I turned to my fiancé and asked, "Is skiing always as this hair-raising?"

He said, "No, you've just been unlucky."

With the slopes closed we had some time to kill before dinner. We had a hot chocolate brandy at the bar and decided that we would go out for a walk.

Two women from my ski lesson were at the bar and overheard us and asked if they could join us. We finished our drinks and started to walk along the path from the back of the hotel. We managed to follow the path, but the further we got into the forest around the hotel, the path disappeared.

The snow was now up to or knees and one of the ladies walking with us had a bad leg so we had to support her under her arms the rest of the way. This made walking slower under the heavy snow conditions. What seemed a fun idea at the time was now starting to look like a bad idea.

We were getting hungry and didn't know our way back to the hotel. I looked out into the distance and could see lights. I said, "Let's head towards the streetlights. It should lead us to a main road."

We finally reached the main road and walked along until we came to some shops.

We had walked quite a way from the hotel and being so tired, we got a cab back to the hotel. We were so thankful to be back and we made it just in time for dinner.

The next couple of days were not so extreme. I now, was able to ski with my fiancé rather than being in the ski school. It had been an experience that I would never forget but one week thrown in the deep end was enough for me. I was proud that I had faced my fears and had managed to ski and complete a run. What stood out for me the most was how patient my fiancé was.

Back home I shared the pictures of our trip with my girls.

People started to ask when we were planning to get married.

My fiancé had mentioned that he wanted his best mate as his best man, the one that had kissed me at the airport. There was no way I could get married knowing what he had done. I could not live with it any longer so I met my fiancé and decided to tell him the truth of what happened and hoped that he would not lose his mate over it.

I did not know what to expect and didn't know how he would react.

I sat down on his sofa and told him what had happened.

He said he needed some space to think.

I never heard from him for a week.

When I did hear from him he told me that he was going away and could not be in the relationship anymore. He still just blanked me and I didn't know where I stood.

One minute I was his fiancé then next thing I was dropped like a tone of bricks with no explanation why. I didn't know what he was thinking. He just went silent.

I didn't even know when he had planned to go away or for how long.

So much for the next forty years of my life being easy. I thought it was too good to be true.

219

I wouldn't mind. I hadn't done anything wrong. it was his best mate who made a pass at me. At the time I could not make a scene because he was giving me a lift home, I just wanted to get home and deal with it after.

My now ex-fiancé sent me a text saying he was leaving in the early hours of the morning, and getting on a flight to Canada for three weeks. He said he just needed some space to get his head together.

The next morning I woke up to a bunch of flowers on my doorstep and some gifts for us all. I thought it was a lovely gift to wake up to and he must still have feelings for us. You would not bother leaving gifts if you didn't.

I felt emotionally floored and my eye had flared up, just to top it off.

This made it hard for me to do my coursework for college.

I just felt in limbo, as I didn't know the outcome and what to expect next.

I focused on my coursework over the next three weeks.

I did hear from him a couple of times while he was away and he told me that he was missing me and wanted to see me for a chat when he got home.

He texted me when he had landed on home turf and asked if we could meet up the next day.

I said, "Yes, no problem. But let's meet at the local pub on neutral territory."

We met and had a drink and he told me that he had time to process everything and that he had felt overwhelmed from being single for so many years and living on his own to suddenly being around so many people.

"Regarding what happened with my so-called friend, I believe you. He has a reputation for trying it on with the women."

I felt so relieved that he believed me and not cross for the fallout this now caused with his friend.

He had lent this so-called friend a lot of money and we later found out that he had borrowed money from many of his friends and disappeared without paying anyone back.

We carried on from where we left off and continued our journey being engaged.

I felt sad that my fiancé had to find out the hard way who his true friends were.

You think you know someone until something changes everything.

We continued getting to know one another and made sure our relationship grew without outside influences getting in the way.

I started to get concerned about my eldest daughter, as she looked burnt out.

She felt faint and had no energy.

I took her to the hospital for some check ups and they admitted her for exhaustion.

I hadn't realized the stress she had been under with her relationship and work.

When she was well enough to leave the hospital she decided that her health was more important.

She left were she worked and split up from her relationship.

She had six months out and had two pence to her name.

One day she was sitting at our computer with our chi on her lap and had a brain wave.

She decided that she wanted to get a loan to open her own shop. She had experience and felt she could make a go of it.

Within a couple of months she had gone from nothing to signing a contract with a business partner with a five year lease on a shop. Her shop needed painting and decorating. Their goal was for it to be open in time for Christmas.

She had met a man and they became an item.

In the meantime, everything else in our family was running smooth. We had set a date for our marriage for the following year at Gretna Green. The focus was on the opening of the shop. We all followed the journey and helped where we could.

The shop opened just in time for Christmas, and her business was welcomed in the community.

With our lives back on track, we celebrated the New Year with optimism.

Later that evening my eldest daughter turned up with her boyfriend and told me that they had something to share with us. She told us that she had found out that she was pregnant. We congratulated them both and we hugged and kissed each other.

They then left after having a drink to go and tell his parents.

Once the news had sunk in and they had time to process it, they both got excited and enjoyed the pregnancy.

My daughter had only known him for three months and felt it couldn't be worse timing with the opening of the shop. I reassured her that many women out there have careers and children.

My daughter didn't like change and had often said to me, "I don't want to grow up."

Her pregnancy grew while she worked hard with her shop. Her boyfriend moved into our house and they shared a room with my youngest. It wasn't ideal but we didn't have any spare rooms. I had the small room and my other two daughters had the biggest room.

I felt sorry for my youngest as she hadn't had a proper bedroom yet. Our situation wouldn't allow it. I had to tell them that they would have to move out, as there simply wasn't enough room for everyone in our house. My daughter moved out and moved in with her partner to his family home. I cried my eyes out not coping with the changes that were occurring to our once just-us-girls life.

I wasn't prepared for our lives to be turned upside down so soon. I thought it would be years away until that day would come. I did not know how to handle this. It felt like my family nest was falling apart. My youngest was still at senior school and in my head, I thought one became a grandparent once all the children had become independent. I wasn't thinking rationally. I was thinking emotionally.

My daughter was fed up with commuting from the area of Kent to work and decided that she wanted to move back closer to be near her family home. She managed to find a flat within walking distance to her place of work and her job paid enough for her to afford the rent.

She and her partner were busy with building their own nest, preparing for the birth of their first baby.

Our wedding was a few days before her due date and sadly she decided, understandably, that she would not be going to our wedding.

We had booked our honeymoon to go to Disneyland in Florida, but we had to have our honeymoon before our marriage because of the school holidays. My youngest would be going on honeymoon with us.

We had the best time of our lives. It may not have been a traditional romantic honeymoon but we loved every minute of it.

When we got back from our honeymoon, with the help of our girls, we started making preparations for our wedding day. We managed to make my bouquet of flowers for four pounds. We made button- holes from plastic flowers. I bought my dress on sale. We managed to find a reasonably priced hotel for our guests who would travel with us to Gretna Green. Our wedding cost was just over a thousand pounds, which included everything.

We bought a cake to cut from a local shop and had Chinese food at a nearby restaurant. We could not have wished for a better wedding. I knew my eldest daughter was with us in our hearts. I was just concerned about missing the birth of their baby.

We arrived home and unpacked and washed clothes and waited patiently for any news.

Finally I got a call to say she was at the hospital and that she had been asking for me and wanted me there at the birth. We turned up and I was shown into the room where the birthing pool was. Before I entered, the midwife told me to keep calm as she was close to giving birth. I quietly walked into the room and stroked her head as she started to give birth. The baby started to go into distress and so they helped my daughter out of the birthing pool, as they had to get her baby out quickly. With water everywhere I held my daughter as she leant her head into my chest, then suddenly her child was born and the midwife cleared the airways.

As they cleaned up their baby, they cleaned my daughter up so she could lie down on the bed. Suddenly the room was filled with the sound of a crying baby and the midwife said, "Congratulations on the birth of your baby boy," and placed him on my daughter's chest.

It was the most surreal experience and gave me an insight on how a partner feels watching a birth.

It can feel quite traumatic when you don't feel in control.

It is something I will never forget and I was thankful mummy and baby were well.

Life had turned another page, with our family expanding in numbers. I now had to get used to being a nanny as well as a mummy.

I had no clue what it was like be a nan. I was still learning each day being a mum.

We left the hospital and shared the pictures of our new grandson.

We were solely dependent on my new husband's wages. I knew that I had to get a job but something inside of me felt that I should not get one yet, because I felt there was something else that I needed to do, but I didn't know what yet. I asked my husband to trust me, as I felt that it would come to me.

We helped our eldest daughter with homemade meals and getting them anything they needed from the shop to help support them through those early weeks with a new baby.

I had been used to loving my four daughters but having a grandson was nothing like I had experienced before. I didn't even know how you would change a boy's nappy.

I started to feel nervous and not as confident as I had felt with my own children.

I started to feel like a nervous nelly and could not tell anyone how I felt as they would think I was nuts having had four of my own children already.

I was mindful not to interfere. I wanted to help and support them but knew how important it was to give them space so they could find their own feet without me getting in the way.

I just thought of the saying *Too many cooks spoil the broth.*

My youngest still needed me and my day revolved around dropping and picking her up from school. After school, my husband was a taxi when she needed to be dropped off anywhere.

My eldest daughter had decided to go back to work.

She had made arrangements with childcare.

She had a work trip coming up and asked me if I would look after him during the day for a week. I agreed and as much as I loved having him, it felt like I equally had a phobia with responsibility. It was the dread of if anything were to happen to him by accident in my care. I panicked when on my own but was ok when another adult was around.

I just didn't want the responsibility on my own. I was tired and life had taken its toll. It felt like my life was catching up with me. I felt a complete failure for how I felt, but I just had not had a break from the responsibility of bringing my own children up without more.

I must be the only one who feels like this as I watch other nannies and they seem laughing and confident without any worry.

I wished I could be like that but I was not.

It pained me to be honest but it's the truth and I won't deny the truth.

I would do anything for my family but even I had some physical limits and had to admit that I am human too.

It was nothing personal and it wasn't because I didn't love my grandson. I just had a problem with more responsibility than I could handle.

In my line of work, having people's lives in your hands is a huge responsibility too. I take my job seriously and give all my energy to the best of my ability.

I had a choice to make. Do I put my energy into my work or not?

I decided it was time and I made the decision to keep my promise to my ex-husband.

I told my husband and he said he would support me with what I needed to do. I started to write daily for about six weeks.

Finally the manuscript was finished. The title of the book would be *From Both Sides of the Fence, The Gifts in U*. I was so proud of myself for completing it and keeping my promise. This book was published a year and a half later.

My second eldest daughter had met a man and had been seeing him for about a year.

We met up with her and her partner and it was while we were out, that she told us that she was pregnant. We were so happy for them both and helped support them as much as we were able.

She lived with her partner at his family home, but soon after finding out about their pregnancy she had found a flat to rent. We helped them move in and to decorate it.

With my second daughter now settled in her own home, we waited for the arrival of their baby.

We were excited about having another grandchild.

We heard that she had to have a caesarean so we all went to the hospital to wait for news. A little while later, her partner came out to let us know that they had a baby boy. We were now proud grandparents to two beautiful grandsons. Our family had changed so much in the space of three years.

With my book now published I knew that I should look for a job. I went back to delivering catalogues through people's doors but the wages were so minimal for the hours that I worked. It wasn't enough to help support my husband with the bills.

I then called in to a local café to see if they had any jobs going. I told them that I had experience as a waitress and making starters for a pub. They took my details and told me that they would contact me if a position became available.

A week later I got a phone call from the café offering me a job, but first they wanted me to come in for a trial. I was actually really nervous about starting as I had been writing my book and been out of touch with working outside my home.

I settled in well and at first they offered me five days a week, but I wanted to still be able to do my psychic readings. So I cut my days to three days a week so I had two days a week to do my readings.

I loved my job and loved the people that I met while at work.

It was handy as I got free bread at the end of the day to take home with me.

About a year later our boss told us that they were selling the shop, and they were giving us about two weeks notice. I was gutted. I knew that I would miss everyone that I had met.

Trying to find a job at my age was not very easy. With no luck at finding a job, my eldest daughter gave me some advice. She said, "Mum, now that your children have grown up, you have the time to do what you love. You're a natural psychic. Instead of looking for work and doing your readings part-time why don't you do what you love full-time?"

I must admit she did have a point, as it was my life's passion. I had been so used to keeping my psychic abilities on the sideline in my life, while I got on with basic every day living that I never really considered having it as a career.

In the meantime, my eldest daughter had to leave where she was living, so she came back to live at home with us. My third daughter moved in with her boyfriend, so that her eldest sister could have her room with her son, while her partner went back home to live with his family.

My second oldest daughter also had to move out of her flat because it was damp and so she came back to live at home, but had to have the lounge as we had no spare bedrooms. We made up their beds every evening. Our house was full to the bursting point but we managed. My husband took it all in stride and was a good sport about the whole situation.

After about four months, my second eldest daughter got another flat around the corner and moved in with her son. Nine months to a year later my eldest daughter moved out and into a house with her son and her partner moved in with them.

My third daughter moved back home and had the small bedroom while my youngest daughter had the largest bedroom.

My youngest had been patient for so many years waiting to have her own bedroom so we decided that she could choose how she wanted to do it up. We took her out to choose paint and a new bed. It was lovely to see her have her own space.

With everyone now settled, it gave me a chance to focus on my work.

My third daughter had gone back to college in the evenings around her full-time job to learn hairdressing.

I became her model for her to practice on. She took it really easily and passed her exams.

I was happy as I now had my own hairdresser in the family.

My eldest daughter told me to start using social media for my work and she showed me how to post on the different platforms.

I just stuck to the basics.

My second daughter managed my readings and booking them in, which freed me up to concentrate on doing the readings without having to worry about the management side.

We decided to do a question and answer evening live over Facebook and Twitter, and this was a success so we arranged to do them every few months.

My youngest daughter left school and went to college. Halfway through, she decided to leave because the coursework wasn't for her. She found a job locally and worked hard to work her way up to a position that she wanted.

My second daughter met a new partner and soon after found out that she was pregnant and had a beautiful baby girl. My daughter was no longer able to manage my readings because of family commitments, so I had to learn to do it on my own.

They later moved into their own home where they are settled and loving life.

My eldest sold her half of her shop and went on to create a new business and became partners with her friend.

I went on to write my second book, *Connecting to Life's Compass; You're Not Lost, You Just Think You Are*, which I got published two years after writing it.

I then met my new guide the end of December 2016. He explained to me that I would be doing soul readings and that I would have to give up doing traditional readings.

I started doing soul readings 1st January 2017.

In 2018, my youngest decided that she wanted to go travelling around Australia.

My third daughter had done it three years earlier and I found her leaving to travel on her own very hard to deal with.

I cried for a whole week until I realized when I spoke to her on Skype that she was actually loving life so what was I crying about?

I found Christmas without her very hard and I didn't feel the same about celebrating or going over the top.

She came back home after four months. I was so pleased that I wouldn't be missing her birthday too.

My youngest worked hard and saved every penny. She was serious and even sold things that she felt she would no longer need.

As a family, we saw her off at the airport, like we had done for her sister previously. I did cry happy tears, as I knew she was made for it. It was in her blood, it was in her soul.

It was now just my husband and me, living at home with my third daughter and our three Chihuahuas.

My third daughter recently got engaged and was making plans for her future.

I then went on to write another book called *The Map of The Universe; A Traveler's Guide.*

Once I had completed this, I then wrote my next booklet, *Soul Disclosure; 100% Access.*

This brings me up to the present day. My work has connected me to people from all around the world.

What love has taught me is that it all works out in the end.

You can fall to the floor many times, and even if you want to give up and cry out in pain, you can but you've got to get back up.

The magic of love is that everyone is the same.

We all have a skeleton and we all have skin.

What defines us in not the colour of our flesh or how tall or short we are or how big or small.

Not even the amount in our banks, as we take none of it with us when we leave here.

We own nothing in material here. In truth everything is loaned to us for however long that we need it.

We all have to let go of everything here, ready to hand it down to the souls that have yet to have their own experiences.

I used to be obsessed at how my body looked.

I was desperate to fit in and for years I had tried going that extra mile to be included and accepted.

I had made sure that I stayed slim even if it meant starving myself or through making myself sick.

It was a full-time job trying to be physically perfect, something that I didn't achieve.

Some things I wasn't able to change like my broad shoulders and my squint.

I had to give up wearing glasses soon after I got married because of my episcleritis symptoms.

I was nervous to face the world with glasses on, as I had been teased so much as a child.

In the end I had to weigh it up. If people only liked me for how I do or don't look then they are not worth having as friends.

Instead of trying to people please and fit in with the world, I decided to fit in my own little world.

I bought a pillow with these words on it and they summed me up nicely.

I know I'm in my own little world but they know me here.

I may have looked like a social drop out and recluse but what I was doing was concentrating on myself to do my work, which took me ten years to do.

If I had not done this then I would not have been able to write the books that I have, as there are too many distractions out there.

Now that I have had this time to complete these books, I am now ready to travel around the world rather than doing it from my living room.

I am ready for the new paradigm. My reason for writing these books was to help guide those who are still trying to figure out their lives.

Life in the physical is like a maze but once you get past your physical self then you see the bigger picture past your flesh and bones and realize you are so much more than your sexual organs.

You will realize that the things you were once hung up about won't bother you anymore.

You may have your sexual organs now but when you exit this earth you don't take them with you.

So who are you?

Are you your gender?

What defines you after all?

Look within and do some soul searching. Then you will find all the answers to yourself and love yourself unconditionally.

OVERVIEW

When I was growing up I thought love was sex. Being starved of love I could not get enough of sex as it meant I was being loved.

I realized that it didn't feel that great and that it was more to do with the ideal view that I had about love like it had been portrayed in the films.

Experiencing sex I soon noticed how sex could be temperamental.

Even if the thought was there it was no guarantee that the action would follow or vise versa.

I had been taught at school during sex education that you had to be careful in case you got pregnant.

Age and different factors can cause disruptions in sex that often feel out of our control.

We are not taught how to feel, just what to do and how to act.

Thinking too much can cause blocks and barriers.

Sex education focuses mainly on protection to stop pregnancy.

To me real sex education should be about communication.

It hasn't helped that in past generations the attitude was to shut up and don't say anything in fear of upsetting someone but how are you meant to connect with your full body if you're only taught to focus on your organs?

How can anyone let themselves go if their mind is hung up with insecure thoughts?

How can anyone relax during sex if you're hung up on how you look and not confident in your own skin?

Sex is more than performance or endurance; it is about reading each other without the need to speak.

We buy so much in life that there is little need in which to give from ourselves.

Past generations would make things with their bare hands with blood and sweat.

Making everyday items so they would last, work was a skill. Now it is about how much you can earn in money rather than quality.

We often say, *If I knew then what I know now I would change so much and not worry so much or take myself so seriously.*

Wise words are often spoken but they fall on ears that do not want to listen.

Wise words are written but they fall on eyes that do not want to read.

Time runs fast so we end up living on empty.

You have more control than you think if you stop what you are doing and observe.

Life can run away with us. My life started out in my search for love and has taken me to where I am now.

I didn't stop when I found my self- love. I didn't stop when I shared my love. I didn't stop when I had everything that I needed in my life.

I felt, what is the point in knowing all this knowledge if I don't share it? This is why I took ten years out of my life to gather all this wisdom and write it over five books so that I could share it with you.

I didn't share it because I wanted to make money. I didn't share it to be a celebrity. I shared it because I love you all and wanted you to have access to your 100% knowledge.

This is the route I took. In sharing it, I trust it may guide you to understand why you are here.

This is the real me. My soul face speaks my truth, as the physical can be selective and hide what you really feel deep down inside. I don't wear my heart on my sleeve; I wear my unconditional soul of infinite love.

You are real and you have feelings and you have thoughts that may at times run away with you.

Luckily for you, you have a soul that will put the breaks on the physical when you need it.

This may mean that you lose your job or you get ill. Whatever sudden event happens, it is not by mistake and it is to get your attention.

If I had not had my children when I did, I would have self-imploded.

I would have pushed my own self-destruct button. I wouldn't have needed anyone else to do it for me.

On paper, I looked a mess and an accident waiting to happen with so many marriages and so many children. I would have been written off before my time.

I wasn't stupid I knew how I looked and how I was judged.

The secret is this:

If you cannot see yourself and if you can't find what you are looking for then don't give up, you create it for yourself. Then you will see yourself in your own creation.

You will not be able to sum me up in one word or many.

You will see many sides to me and many angles.

I can be whatever you want me to be and I can equally be what I choose for me.

I had let others rule and dictate my life for so many years. I chose to believe what they saw in me. I forgot to actually look for myself, so I could make my own mind up.

This is self- responsibility.

If you don't like how other people treat you, then don't hang around with them.

You have a choice to walk away and move on.

The reason why people hold on to situations and relationships that no longer benefit them is because they are scared of being alone with themselves.

To be scared of yourself is to be scared of your life.

Well, I certainly wasn't scared of myself and so this gave me the strength to face myself eventually.

I had already had the heads up of how shit I was so I knew there couldn't be anything worse than what I had already experienced.

What did I have to lose?

Nothing.

I was scared of failing my children and not being good enough for them or not matching up to their expectations.

But I did not fear it.

With so many children, at times I didn't know my head from my toes.

I had just finished tuning in to give guidance to one of my children and I would just sit down and I would be asked to tune in by another.

The transition into soul mummy was subtle because my soul side grew with them.

At first my children needed me as their physical mummy, a mummy that tied shoelaces and made sure they had all the practical things for everyday life.

As they grew up they needed guidance to reassure their minds, they needed guidance with decisions and guidance to calm their nerves.

With so many children needing my psychic abilities more than my physical ones,

I started to turn into soul mummy full-time.

To look at me, I hadn't changed. I still looked the same.

I just didn't talk to them from my physical perspective or reaction. I always spoke to them with my soul knowing.

It changed my lifestyle and it meant I would not be the physical mummy that they had grown up with but they had more of me that they would need.

I was thankful that I didn't give up on love or written myself off like many may have.

If I hadn't been open to love then I would not have met my amazing husband.

He has never judged me or abused me. He has always supported me and trusted me. I thank him for supporting my work. Without him, these books would not have been published.

This last chapter in my life taught me that just because I had grown out of being a child, it didn't mean I had to kill of my childlike spirit.

Just because I had grown into an adult it didn't mean that I should stop having fun and not laugh anymore.

It seemed to me that becoming an adult meant you had to be self-conscious and if you let your hair down it meant you had something wrong with you.

Having my children so young meant I didn't have time to become an adult where I lost my child like spirit.

I kept my spirit alive so I could relate to my children through their eyes rather than the view of only an adult.

I knew when to have my sensible head on but I equally knew how to let my hair down.

I did not want to turn into an adult if it meant giving up the joy of fun and laughter. I chose to multi-task and only give up the labels that didn't define me.

I made many mistakes along the way because as much as I live from my soul, dealing with people is unpredictable and can catch you off guard.

I am still part physical because my soul is connected to my flesh by my breath, I will not let go of it until I take my last breath.

So I have spent my life not learning and being taught about the physical subjects of the world.

I focused on how to master my physical self so I could live infinitely free rather than in limited distortion.

When I was going through adversity when my life looked hopeless,

I would sit and look at my life and search for one thing that I could be thankful for and appreciate it in my life.

I knew that if the day ever came where I could not find one thing to appreciate then I knew my life was over.

This never had happened as I always found four things that I was thankful for, and that I appreciated.

It was my four daughters and so I knew that no matter how dire my life got I had four shining souls in my life giving me the strength to stand up and keep going.

If you cannot appreciate one thing in your life then you will not appreciate many.

I vowed to always treat every reading that I ever did as my first, that way I would always see the magic in it and not get complacent.

Love is within you as it is around you; love is what makes life come alive.

Without love you would not experience anything.

When love touches you – you never forget it.

I started my life in the shadow of pain that was carried by people that I met.

I stopped listening to the dictation of abuse and control and instead started to listen to the guidance of my feelings and not my mind.

Love is a thread that connected all my family together.

Finding yourself is to connect with your self.

Like the universe itself, it is always expanding, as there is never an end or a final chapter. There is always more to add to what you already remember.

Everything is a reflection of the self.

This made me think back to when my children's father said they would grow up to hate me, thankfully they didn't and we have a bond that is love strong.

What he saw was his own reflection and not about me after all.

If only I had known that then rather than carrying that worry for so many years, waiting until they had grown up and reached past eighteen.

They say be careful what you wish for.

Your reality is what you think, what you speak and how you act.

Your reality is of your own making and there is no one to blame, for you are your own master.

If we were all born with no knowledge of gender or of image, we would all connect and share how we felt with no judgment or opinions because we would not know any differently.

I have no preference how you apply your physical body and how you use it, how you master it is a whole different ballgame.

You can live in the shallow end and you can live in the deep end but they both are still part of the same body of water.

Just one is expanded and more open and vast than the other.

You have a choice to go through life and close yourself off, or to go through life selecting parts while missing so much, or choosing to expand so you can see the bigger picture.

If you have wondered, *Is there more to life than what I see?* Then you know you are ready to explore more of who you are.

You are full of love. It is up to you how much of it you access and how much of it you share.

To give up on love is to give up on your
Self!

EPILOGUE

You may still wonder *how is love in everything?*

It is because love is every emotion and feeling.

To know if you like something or hate it or even love it, first you have to experience it to confirm it.

It does not come from the word itself as it can be given more than one label.

Feelings that you associate with words, give it depth, meaning, and knowing.

Love singles out no one.

Everything and everyone is included in love.

When you start separating and selecting parts of love you then miss the point.

When love is typecast, you can grow into and out of love and back into love.

In truth, we never fall out of love. We have outgrown the experience.

This book is not my total love of life so far, as it is in all my books that I have written.

Each book tells my story from a different perspective and angle.

I started my journey as a baby and grew into a child, a teenager and then an adult. I became a mother and a friend, a wife and a nanny.

I have been many names and many labels and headings. Names do not define me.

I call you 'my loves' for a reason because then I am addressing your totality.

In love, I felt hate and have been laughed at, and laughed with.

In love, I have been blamed and abused, accused, judged and assumed.

In love, I have been manipulated and used.

In love, I have been spoilt and denied, I have been harmed as well as self- harmed.

In love, I have labeled myself as well as been labeled.

In love, I have followed as well as been singled out.

In love, I have been highlighted and invisible.

In love, I have been trusted and distrusted.

In love, I have cried even when I look happy.

In love, I have cried when not sad.

Society stereotypes so that we are recognized without being different.

This book may not give you a fairytale ending a happily ever after, but my life is still a work in progress. So is yours.

It may not be a romantic novel but what I offer is my brutal honesty. What you see in me is what you get.

This is my true and real journey of love.

I may not be qualified with a piece of paper but I am qualified in experience.

I used to worry if people didn't like me or hated me.

Now I have no preference as I recognized that every reaction is a reflection of love.

From a young age, I adapted to life here. First my flesh adapted from being inside the womb to then breathing the air.

I adapted from laying down, to then mastering how to move and stand up.

As I grew, my vocal sounds adapted into words.

We are adapting all the time through each year that we turn with age.

We adjust to the food that we taste and we adjust to atmospheres and adjust to climate.

Nothing stays the same; it just looks like it.

You would have to see life under a microscope to see what the eyes do not see.

I have always looked past the front cover at what is obvious and staring me in the face.

I look past words that are being spoken. I look past actions to find the reason and meaning.

I look past expressions to find the feelings. I look at love from all angles and not through rose-tinted spectacles.

I am deep and intense and I analyze everything. I am curious and want to understand what makes people tick.

I want my life to feel real and authentic rather than an act.

I have my moral ground as my own foundations that I built my life on.

I built my foundations from what I believed in and not from what I thought I should follow to fit in.

The elements of my foundation are as follows:

Love – Inspired by my first experience with my dad.

Truth – Inspired from the lie that I experienced with my mum.

Honesty – Inspired by people not speaking what they really feel.

Respect – Inspired by those that abused me.

Manners – Inspired by those who forgot what quality is.

Confidence – Inspired by those who mentally pulled me apart.

Understanding – Inspired by those who did not take the time to get to know me.

Patience – Inspired me by the magic of sharing.

Teamwork – Inspired by being an orphan.

This created trust naturally in my family as our love covered everything.

These elements of our foundation give us more than the walls of our home; it gives us freedom in our loving space to grow while understanding what unconditional love is.

It is not about being there just on happy days or when you can be treated and rewarded with gifts.

Love is like a flower that grows in the garden; it faces all weather.

From experience all I could do was prepare my children, so they could hold their own for when they became adults.

This had nothing to do with how tall they were or how pretty or whether or not they had the in clothes.

It didn't matter how physically strong they were as it wasn't about fighting your way through life.

What I shared with my children is inner strength.

I wanted them to feel their own inner gold that would set them up for life; that would stay with them through every step and every decision that they would make.

Nurturing their unique selves was more than taking a selfie with a camera. A picture can get destroyed like the flesh and can be torn apart.

No one can touch the magic inside. Only you hold the key to yourself through the energy of your soul.

Master yourself then you master your own reality in unconditional love.

LOVE IS NOT ONE SIDED OR ONE SIDE OF ME
IT IS ALL OF ME
MY QUIRKS
MY STRENGTHS
MY WEAKNESSES
MY VUNERALBILITY
MY INADEQUACIES
THIS IS WHAT MAKES MY LIFE PERFECT AND FULL
OF LOVE.
SO I WILL NEVER FORGET MY CONNECTION WITH
THE TOTALITY OF INFINITE KNOWING.

MUCH LOVE TO YOU DEE XXX

Review Requested:

If you loved this book, would you please provide
a review at Amazon.com and Amazon.co.uk?